The Fast-Track ME

Co-published with AMED (the Association for Management Education and Development)

Consultant Editors
John Kind, Director, Harbridge Consulting Group
David Megginson, Associate Head, Sheffield Business School

THE FAST-TRACK MBA SERIES represents an innovative and refreshingly different approach to presenting core subjects in a typical MBA syllabus in a lively and accessible way. The usual text book approach is eschewed in favour of a practical, action-oriented style which involves the reader in self-assessment and participation.

Ideal for managers wanting to renew or develop their management capabilities, the books in *THE FAST-TRACK MBA SERIES* rapidly give readers a sound knowledge of all aspects of business and management that will boost both self-confidence and career prospects. For those fortunate enough to take an MBA, the *Series* will provide a solid grounding in the subjects to be studied. Managers and students worldwide will find this new series an exciting and challenging alternative to the usual study texts and management guides.

Titles already available in the series are:

★ *Strategic Management* (Robert Grant & James Craig)
★ *Organisational Behaviour and Design* (Barry Cushway & Derek Lodge)
★ *Problem Solving and Decision Making* (Graham Wilson)
★ *Human Resource Development* (David Megginson, Jennifer Joy-Matthews & Paul Banfield)
★ *Accounting for Managers* (Graham Mott)
★ *Human Resource Management* (Barry Cushway)

Forthcoming books in the series will cover:

Data Analysis and IT ★ Financial Management ★ International Management ★ Investment and Risk ★ Law ★ Business Ethics ★ Marketing ★ Operations Management.

AMED is an association of individuals who have a professional interest in the development of people at work. AMED's network brings together people from industry, the public sector, academic organizations and consultancy, and is exclusive to individuals.

The aims of AMED are to promote best practice in the fields of individual and organizational development, to provide a forum for the exploration of new ideas, to offer members opportunities for their development and to encourage the adoption of ethical practices in development.

For further information on AMED you are invited to write to AMED, 14-15 Belgrave Square, London SW1X 8PS.

The Series Editors

John Kind is a director of Harbridge House, a consultancy firm special-
izing in management development and training. He has wide experience of
designing and presenting business education programmes in various parts
of the world for clients such a BAA, Bass, British Petroleum and General
Electric. John Kind is a visiting lecturer at Henley Management College and
holds an MBA from the Manchester Business School and an honours
degree in Economics.

David Megginson is a writer and researcher on self-development and the
line manager as developer. He has written *A Manager's Guide to Coaching*,
Self-development: A Facilitator's Guide, *Human Resource Development* in
the Fast-track MBA series, *The Line Managers as Developer* and the
Developing the Developers research report. He consults and researches in
blue chip companies, and public and voluntary organizations. He is a
director of the European Mentoring Centre and an elected Council member of AMED, and has been Associate Head of Sheffield Business School
and a National Assessor for the National Training Awards.

Macro-
Economics

KEITH WADE

FRANCIS BREEDON

Published in association with  AMED

KOGAN
PAGE

YOURS TO HAVE AND TO HOLD

BUT NOT TO COPY

First published in 1995

Kogan Page Limited
120 Pentonville Road
London N1 9JN

© Keith Wade and Francis Breedon, 1995

British Library Cataloguing in Publication Data

A CIP record for this book is available from the British Library.

ISBN 0 7494 1173 2

Typeset by Saxon Graphics Ltd, Derby
Printed and bound in Great Britain by Biddles Ltd, Guildford and Kings Lynn

Contents

Foreword by Sir John Egan

Every business succeeds by satisfying the needs of its customers. Managers have therefore to refresh continually their understanding of their customers' requirements and anticipate shifts in demand and expectations.

One thing does, however, tend to remain constant. Customers want good quality and low cost. So the managerial challenge is to deliver products and services efficiently, profitably and to high standards of quality so that the enterprise can prosper.

Of course all competitive businesses must also seek to raise continually their standards of customer satisfaction. The market-place continues to widen, and in many sectors is already global, and the cost of entry to markets tends to decrease. Businesses must respond by continuously improving themselves.

These simple, even obvious, principles can be very difficult to put into practice, but in Britain we have now started to learn from the experience of others, such as Germany and Japan, by improving our managerial processes.

The most vital contributor to Continuous Improvement is the manager. All managers have to ensure that their own education and training is sufficient for the business challenges of both today and tomorrow. Relying solely on learning by experience on the job will leave too much to chance. The successful manager of the future will accept responsibility for his or her own development and the development of their staff.

The Fast-Track MBA series should be an invaluable aid to the manager who wants to improve personal performance and to plan for long-term success.

Sir John Egan
Chief Executive, BAA plc

To our wives

Acknowledgements

We would like to thank the many people who have helped us in writing this book, particularly Peter Breedon, David Gasparro and David Mackie who all made invaluable suggestions and Aelred Connelly who produced the charts. Any errors remain our own.

1

Introduction

Macroeconomics is the study of the whole economy. It is primarily concerned with how much the economy can produce and how fast prices will rise in the process. The macroeconomic performance of an economy determines the living standards of its people, and sets the environment in which business operates. While there is little the individual can do to influence this, as the flow of economic information and opinion steadily grows it has become increasingly necessary to be able to interpret economic events.

This can be seen most clearly in the financial markets, which react almost instantaneously to the latest economic releases, but it is also relevant to anyone planning decisions which will have an impact at some point in the future. This is because it is possible for a company with good products, excellent marketing and an apparently sound financial structure to be wrong-footed by a sharp change in demand. Consequently, choosing the right time to invest and expand, or make a strategic acquisition, is often critically dependent on the economic cycle.

The focus of this book is on the factors which determine swings in the economy and how the government is likely to respond. After reading it you should be in a better position to identify the key macroeconomic determinants of demand for your organization's products or services, and how exposed your organization is to the economic cycle. You should then be able to answer critical questions such as, 'Business is going well at the moment, but are the authorities about to raise interest rates, and if so, how would such a move affect demand in the economy?' From this perspective an understanding of macroeconomics is a vital strategic element in business success.

An aim of this book is to take some of the luck out of such decisions by providing a framework for anticipating changes in economic activity. In turn this should enable you to gain a better perspective on how the economy affects your industry, to enable you to exploit economic fluctuations rather than be a casualty of them.

An Example

The impact of macroeconomics on business was brought home most forcibly in the UK in the late 1980s when, after a long period of economic expansion, interest rates were doubled from 7.5 to 15 per cent between May 1988 and October 1989. Companies and households who had borrowed heavily in anticipation of further economic growth were faced with a massive increase in interest payments which cut into their cash flow. The subsequent fall in demand sent the economy into recession. As corporate profitability fell, many firms undertook massive restructuring and unemployment rose sharply. In this environment the key to a firm's survival depended on how exposed it had become to interest rates during the upturn, and how fast it reacted as the economy turned down. On the whole, those who came through had not overextended themselves at the end of the decade, choosing instead to eschew further expansion and borrowing. Many others who had thought that business would carry on growing rapidly went out of business entirely. The government of the day paid the price in terms of a severely reduced majority in the 1992 general election. This example highlights the importance of the economic cycle in determining the success of strategic decisions.

Overview

The book is divided into three parts. In Part One we describe the key factors which influence total demand and supply in the economy. Chapter 2 tackles the demand side where we break expenditure into its key components. By looking at the factors which drive household and corporate spending it is possible to build up a picture of overall demand in the economy. In Chapter 3 we bring in the supply side: the amount of goods and services which the economy is physically able to produce. Economic activity is driven by demand in the short run, but is determined by supply-side factors in the long run. If demand takes the economy beyond its normal ability to supply, then prices take the strain and inflation accelerates. The economy is being overstretched and demand needs to be reined back.

In such a situation we would expect the government to step in and restore equilibrium. The tools it has available to achieve this are discussed in Part Two. These can be divided into taxes and public expenditure (fiscal policy), and interest rates (monetary policy). In Chapter 4 we describe the influences on fiscal policy, and highlight its effect on incentives, as well as the level of demand in the economy. We also look at budget deficits and the constraints they can impose on governments. With fiscal policy being increasingly used to pursue microeconomic aims, interest rates have become the main lever of macroeconomic policy. In Chapter 5, we turn to monetary policy and look at the effectiveness of changes in interest rates on activity. The importance of credibility is also discussed. Not surprisingly, government policy is more effective when people believe it will achieve its aims, and we see how credibility is won and lost. Chapter 6 then focuses on the exchange rate, how it is determined, and why policy makers have tried to use it as a target of economic policy. The overall aim of Part Two is to look at the economy from the viewpoint of the policy-maker, something which is essential for understanding and anticipating changes in monetary and fiscal policy.

The last section of the book, Part Three, then puts into practice the analysis of the previous two parts. Chapter 7 shows how to identify where the economy is now and where it is likely to be heading. The aim is not to describe an entire economic forecast, but to highlight the key factors, so that the reader knows what to look for among the vast supply of data and surveys. This chapter draws on the analysis of Chapters 2 and 3 in determining where the economy is in its cycle, and on Chapters 4 and 5 for assessing the likely policy response. The final chapter then looks at two issues which have taxed economists and policy-makers for most of the twentieth century. First, the choice of exchange rate regime. For example, the UK's recent experience in the European Exchange Rate Mechanism (ERM) has echoes with that of the Gold Standard in the 1930s. Secondly, we discuss the growing problem of unemployment in the developed economies.

This book will not turn the reader into an economist (something in its favour), but should provide a better understanding of the processes which drive the economy.

Analysing activity:
the demand side

The most commonly quoted yardstick of economic performance is Gross Domestic Product (GDP), the volume of goods and services produced by the economy in a given period. The terms boom and slump, recession and recovery all refer to GDP growth, or its absence.

The aims of this chapter are:

1. to show you how GDP is measured;
2. to describe changes in GDP in terms of its components;
3. to identify the demand-side factors which drive GDP.

This is the first part of our analysis of GDP, where we emphasize the factors which influence the amount households and firms wish to spend on goods and services. In other words, we are only focusing on the demand side and are not concerned about possible constraints on domestic production. In the second part of our analysis (in Chapter 3) we will bring in the supply side to take the productive capacity of the economy into account.

Measuring Gross Domestic Product

Nominal and real GDP

There are two measures of GDP, nominal and real. Nominal GDP is the *value* of output at current prices, while real GDP measures the same output at prices in a base year. In this way, real GDP is a measure of the *volume* of output, as it is the value of production adjusted for price changes. Real GDP growth is the change in the volume of goods and services produced in a given period, usually a year. Nominal GDP growth is the change in the value of GDP. Therefore the difference between nominal and real GDP growth is inflation, the change in the price level in a given period.

When we talk about GDP growth we almost always mean the change in real, not nominal, GDP, as this relates to the amount produced by the economy. For example, in 1993 nominal GDP in the UK rose by 5.5 per cent to £630 billion. Of this increase, about two percentage points represented higher production of goods and services (real growth), while the remainder was due to higher prices (inflation).

The circular flow of income

By definition, the total value of goods and services produced by the economy is equal to the total amount which are sold. In turn, this must be equal to total incomes, as the proceeds from sales are used to pay the workforce and owners of the company. Therefore GDP can be measured in three different ways — in terms of production, expenditure or income. This is often referred to as the circular flow of income, as income flows from consumers to producers and then back to households in the form of wages, rent and profits. When statisticians measure GDP they are essentially cutting into this circular flow. In the next section we briefly look at these three measures of GDP.

The output measure

The most direct method of measuring the economy's production (GDP) is to sum the goods and services produced by each sector. The latter are defined as agriculture, construction, energy, manufacturing and the service industries. The contribution of each to GDP is the value of output produced minus the value of inputs into that sector from other sectors, ie the value-added of each sector. If we simply totalled the value of all sales we would overestimate GDP, as the sales of some sectors are used as inputs into the products of others. This is known as double-counting.

For example, the value of sales from the food manufacturing industry includes the cost of inputs from agriculture, which are already included in GDP as part of agricultural production. The contribution of food manufacturing to GDP must exclude this from the value of its final output, if we are to avoid counting the agricultural contribution twice in GDP.

Figure 2.1 shows the contribution of each sector to UK GDP.

The income approach

When output has been produced and suppliers have been paid, firms pay their workforce and shareholders. Thus, wages and profits (the income of workers and the owners of firms) are equivalent to value-added and also sum to GDP. Figure 2.2 shows a breakdown of GDP into components of income.

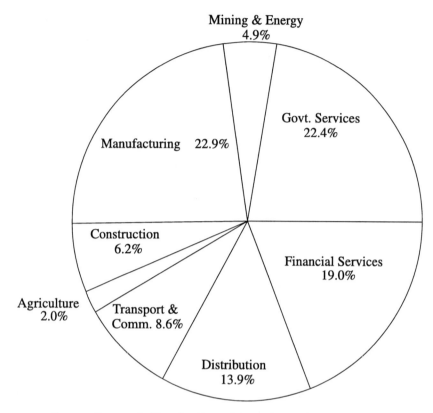

Source: Economic Trends, Central Statistical Office.

Figure 2.1   *Share of UK GDP by sector, 1993*

The expenditure approach

The third method of measuring GDP is to add up the expenditure of those who purchase finished, or final, goods and services. In any given period, the output produced by the economy is either sold at home or abroad or, if unsold, goes into stocks. By adding up this expenditure and including the change in stocks, we obtain the expenditure estimate of GDP. The problem of double-counting is avoided by only considering final sales, and not including expenditure on intermediate goods which go into the production of finished goods and services. Real GDP is obtained from nominal GDP by adjusting (or deflating) the nominal estimates of expenditure by a price index (known as a deflator).

Because it is often easier to think of its determinants, this is the most frequently analysed measure of GDP and involves defining several types of expenditure. These are:

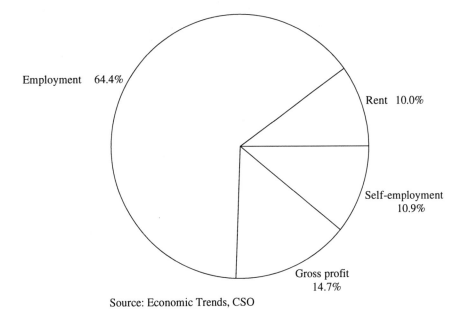

Employment   64.4%

Rent   10.0%

Self-employment
10.9%

Gross profit
14.7%

Source: Economic Trends, CSO

Figure 2.2   *Share of UK GDP by income, 1993*

■ *Consumers' expenditure* which represents household spending on goods, such as cars, furniture, food, clothing and footwear, and services such as travel fares, rent, rates, insurance and telephone charges. This is normally the largest component of GDP in an economy.

■ *Government consumption* which includes expenditure on military defence, the National Health Service, education and other government services which are mainly paid for indirectly through taxation.

■ *Fixed investment* includes expenditure on plant and equipment, construction projects (both private and public) and personal sector investment in housing.

■ *Stockbuilding* covers goods which are produced but unsold. Although there has been no expenditure on this category, as they have been made in the economy they need to be included in GDP. Note that it is the change in stock levels that is included in GDP, so that stockbuilding can make a positive or negative contribution.

The sum of consumer spending, government consumption, fixed investment and stockbuilding gives *domestic expenditure* — total domestic demand by residents of the economy in a given period. Adding *exports*, goods and services which are produced in the country concerned but sold abroad, to domestic expenditure gives *total final expenditure*.

Some of this expenditure will include purchases of goods produced overseas, *imports*. These need to be deducted from total final expenditure to leave expenditure on domestically produced goods and services, *GDP at market prices*. We can also deduct the value of taxes and subsidies which are included in expenditure at market prices to leave *GDP at factor cost*.

In practice, each category of expenditure is first measured in nominal terms and then adjusted into real terms by using estimates of the change in price.

GDP is often written as an equation:

$$\text{GDP} = C + I + G + (X - M)$$

where: C is consumers' expenditure
I is fixed investment and stockbuilding
G is government consumption
X is exports
M is imports

Table 2.1 shows the expenditure components of GDP for the UK.

Analysing GDP

The expenditure approach to measuring real GDP provides the framework for most analysis and forecasts of the economy. Each component is evaluated and then combined with the other elements of expenditure to give GDP. The change in GDP in each period can

Table 2.1   *The expenditure components of UK GDP, 1993 (£ billion)*

Consumers' expenditure	405.6	
Government consumption	138.2	
Fixed investment	94.7	
Stockbuilding	–0.2	
Domestic expenditure		638.4
Exports	158.0	
Total final expenditure		796.4
less Imports	166.3	
Statistical discrepancy	–0.1	
Gross Domestic Product (market prices)		630.0
less Taxes plus subsidies	83.9	
Gross Domestic Product (factor cost)		546.1

Source: *UK National Accounts (The Blue Book 1994)*, Central Statistical Office

then be broken down into changes in expenditure, so that we can determine the mix of growth, and identify what is driving activity.

Real GDP rose by 2 per cent in the UK in 1993, led by an increase in consumer spending which contributed over 1.6 percentage points to the rise. When combined with an increase in investment (including stockbuilding) overall domestic demand was worth more than 2 percentage points of growth. Exports also added to growth, but these increases were offset by a rise in imports so that overall GDP was limited to a 2 per cent rise.

Demand Analysis

Breaking down changes in real GDP in this way gives a useful arithmetic description of growth. We now need to look at the factors which drive the components of expenditure. At this stage we only consider how much households, firms and the government wish to spend on goods and services — known as total or aggregate demand. We do not take into account the ability of the economy to meet this demand, and are effectively assuming that there are no constraints on production. In the next chapter we relax this assumption and introduce the supply side of the economy.

Consumption

Consumer spending and government consumption are often collectively referred to as consumption, as they largely comprise goods and services which are consumed shortly after purchase.

Consumer spending

Consumer spending is the largest component of aggregate expenditure, accounting for nearly two-thirds of domestic demand in the UK (see Table 2.1). Clearly, fluctuations in consumption can have a major influence on demand and national output, and are one of the key components of any forecast. Indeed, the accuracy of the consumer spending predictions often determines the success of the overall forecast.

Key determinants

1. Real Personal Disposable Income (RPDI).
2. Savings.

In any period the amount of goods and services which people consume will depend on their real disposable income (nominal income after tax, adjusted for price increases) and whether they wish to add to, or reduce, their savings. Strong increases in real income may not translate into strong spending if households decide they would rather be increasing their savings. Therefore to analyse the outlook for consumer spending we need to consider the prospects for real income growth and the factors which influence savings.

Disposable income is the most important determinant of the level of consumption. For every £100 received as disposable income by the personal sector in the UK in 1993, just under £88 was spent. However, changes in savings behaviour can have large effects at the margin and are a key determinant of consumption growth. For example in 1992, if consumers had chosen to spend all of the increase in their real disposable income, consumer spending would have risen by nearly 3 per cent. Instead, the increase in income went into savings and consumption remained flat. This was sufficient to keep the overall economy in the doldrums.

In the next section we describe the main influences on real personal disposable income and savings.

Influences on real personal disposable income

It is useful to break RPDI into four components:

Real Personal Disposable Income (RPDI)
=   Income from employment and other income
    plus social security benefits
    minus taxes
    adjusted for price increases

Income from employment tends to be the most important factor in disposable income growth, increasing rapidly when activity is strong and employment and wages are rising, but falling back during recessions when unemployment increases and pay moderates. Other income mainly consists of net interest and dividend receipts and will move in line with interest rates (mortgage payments are in this category) and profits in the economy. Benefits and taxes generally play a stabilizing role, helping to cushion the impact of higher unemployment on income during a downturn, while taxes rise more rapidly during periods of strong expansion as rising incomes take people into higher tax brackets.

Large increases in wages and salaries add little to spending power if they are offset by equivalent increases in prices. Therefore, to find the real amount people have available to spend on goods and services, disposable income needs to be reduced by the increase in prices.

Influences on saving

Permanent Income The theory of savings begins with the idea that people prefer a stable level of consumption, rather than feast today and famine tomorrow. The gains during times of plenty do not compensate for the loss during periods of shortage. If people experience a temporary fall in their income they are likely to maintain their spending by running down savings or borrowing, knowing that savings balances can be replenished or borrowing repaid when income returns to normal. Only if the income loss is thought to be permanent will consumption be cut, as people then recognize that their previous level of spending is now unsustainable.

Permanent income is not something that can be easily measured as it depends on people's perceptions of their future income. Nevertheless, two factors provide a useful guide. The first is the state of the jobs market, or more precisely the trend in unemployment. If unemployment is rising, people in work may become concerned about the prospect of losing their job and save more as a precaution against becoming unemployed. In other words, they reduce their present consumption as their expectations about future income fall.

Secondly, house prices and share values are good indicators of expected income. House prices generally move steadily in line with income growth, but if people then believe that their incomes will grow significantly faster, they will expect prices to be higher in the future and will be prepared to pay more for a house now. Thus house prices will temporarily rise above their long-term relationship to current income, reflecting an increase in permanent income expectations. Similarly, share prices will rise when the prospects for profits, and hence payments to shareholders, improve.

Rising asset values suggest that income expectations have risen, and that consumers are prepared to save less as they are more confident about their future incomes. Borrowing is the means by which people can realize such an improvement in their permanent income expectations, without having to wait for those expectations to be fulfilled. Thus, increases in borrowing combined with rising asset prices indicate an improvement in permanent income expectations and lower savings.

Interest Rates Imagine that people's expectations of their future income have improved, households have become more confident about their job prospects and house prices are rising — then the decision to spend more will depend on the level of interest rates.

Interest rates are the trade-off in choosing to consume today rather than tomorrow. Households can either spend their income today or save it, earn interest and have more to spend in a year's time. When interest rates rise, the returns from saving increase and there is a greater incentive to reduce current expenditure. For those households whose expenditure exceeds their income, higher interest rates create an incentive to reduce borrowing and cut back on consumption.

In choosing whether to consume today or tomorrow, the consumer will also consider the likely price of the desired goods in the future. If prices are expected to rise rapidly, then even if interest rates are high, the consumer may be better off by buying the goods now (even if they have to borrow) rather than paying a higher price in the future. It is the difference between nominal interest rates and expected price inflation, known as the *real interest rate*, which determines the incentive to borrow and spend, rather than forgo consumption and save.

Table 2.2 gives a numerical example of how interest rates and inflation influence the return to saving.

Table 2.2 *The return to saving: number of goods which can be bought in one year's time*

		0	10	20
		Interest rate (% per annum)		
Inflation rate				
(% per annum)	20	8.3	9.2	10.0
	10	9.1	10.0	10.9
	0	10.0	11.0	12.0

In this example we assume that a household can either consume 10 units of a good at a price of £1 each today, or save £10 for one year and buy the number of goods shown in the cells of the matrix.

When the interest rate equals inflation, the interest earned from saving is matched by a rise in price, so the consumer can still buy 10 units in one year's time and is no better or worse off from saving. The real interest rate, the return to saving, is zero. When interest rates exceed inflation, households can buy more than ten units in one year's time, so the return to saving is positive. Conversely, when the interest rate is below the rate of inflation, the household is worse off by saving.

Table 2.3 summarizes the key influences on consumer spending.

Table 2.3 *The key determinants of consumers' expenditure*

Employment Wages Other income Taxes Inflation	Real Personal Disposable Income	
		Consumer spending
Permanent income – Job security – Asset prices Real interest rate – nominal rate minus inflation	Saving	

Government consumption

Government consumption accounts for about one-fifth of domestic expenditure in the UK (see Table 2.1), and includes expenditure on defence, health, education and other government services which are used by the personal sector. These items are separated out from consumers' expenditure as they are mainly paid for through taxation rather than being bought at market prices. In the absence of a measure of market value, the wage bill for these services is used to value their contribution to GDP.

The amount spent in this category largely reflects the political priorities of the government and the state of its finances. Government consumption can also be used as a lever to alter the level of overall demand in the economy. For example, in the past governments have tried to boost domestic demand by raising expenditure. We examine these issues in Chapter 4 on fiscal policy.

Investment

Fixed investment and stockbuilding account for a smaller proportion of domestic demand than does consumption; however, investment is more volatile and so can often outweigh consumption in its impact on demand and GDP. For example, in the UK in 1990 domestic demand fell as cuts in investment outweighed a rise in consumption. Further reductions in investment deepened the recession in 1991. This volatility makes investment a key part of the growth forecast.

Fixed investment

Fixed capital formation is more fully referred to as Gross Domestic Fixed Capital Formation: 'gross' because nothing is deducted for wear and tear (depreciation), and 'domestic' as it only relates to investment within the boundary of the economy. We refer to it simply as fixed investment.

The private sector accounts for over 80 per cent of fixed investment in the UK, with government projects making up the remainder. In the national accounts investment is also broken down into four asset categories: vehicles, ships and aircraft, plant and machinery, dwellings and other new building and works. Plant and machinery is usually the largest category, accounting for over a third of the total.

Thus, in addition to its role in demand, fixed investment also represents the gross addition to the nation's stock of housing, roads, vehicles, offices and plant and equipment. Although it does not capture consumption of capital (depreciation), to the extent that this can be postponed, fixed investment is a measure of changes in the productive capacity of the economy. We explore this further in the next chapter when we look at the supply side of the economy.

Key Determinants

Investment involves spending money now to realize a return in the future. An outlay will only be made if the expected return from the project is sufficient to cover its costs, plus a premium to compensate for the risk that it might go wrong. We can break this down into three key factors:

1.   Expected demand
2.   Cost of capital
3.   Risk

Expected demand
There are often long lead times between the decision to invest and the subsequent increase in productive capacity, so in planning their

capital expenditure companies and the government have to look ahead and anticipate future demand.

This judgement may be made with the help of economic forecasts from the main forecasting bodies, or in-house teams of economists. Projections for GDP are then tailored to the firm's product, taking into account whether demand in that particular area tends to rise more rapidly, or more slowly, than growth in the economy as a whole. In the private sector a company will also take a view on the likely strength of future competition, and hence the scope it will have for setting prices.

In an ideal world, forecasts of future demand would be so accurate that business would be able to invest with a high degree of confidence, such that extra production would come on stream just when it was needed. The firm would never hit full capacity or experience bottlenecks, and investment would be relatively stable, responding to long-run trends in demand, driven by such factors as demographics and new technology.

The actual behaviour of investment suggests we are a long way from this ideal. In practice, capital expenditure tends to be one of the most volatile components of demand, typically rising 20 per cent during an upswing before falling sharply during a downturn. The close correlation with capacity constraints shows that firms tend to wait until they are very close to their production limits before making new investment. This suggests that decision-makers find it difficult to predict future demand accurately, and so wait until capacity is short before deciding to add to it. Such behaviour partly reflects the poor record of economic forecasters, who have missed many of the economy's key turning points, and partly the related failure of successive governments to control demand. It may also be simply due to human nature. Business will only invest if it is sufficiently confident about the future, and this in turn may require that demand is already growing rapidly.

The observation that capital spending tends to strengthen later in the business cycle, after demand has been rising for some time, is exploited in the *accelerator theory of investment*, where the change in GDP during the last year represents expected future demand and drives capital spending.

Another explanation for the very cyclical pattern of investment is that balance sheets tend to be stronger later in the cycle as firms have had a good run of profits. Although in theory each investment project should be judged on its own merits, in practice companies may not have access to capital unless they have reasonably strong finances (see below).

To summarize, expected demand tends to be heavily influenced by current activity, capacity constraints and the state of company finances.

Cost and availability of finance

When expected demand has been determined, this must then be compared with the cost of finance to obtain an overall expected return. Only if the expected return exceeds the cost of finance by a sufficient margin to compensate the company for the risk it is taking will the project proceed.

In seeking the lowest cost of capital companies can consider a wider range of sources than the personal sector. In addition to borrowing from banks they can also tap into the financial markets by issuing equities or bonds. In either case, however, the cost of finance will be directly related to the level of interest rates in the economy. For example, an increase in interest rates would raise the cost of equity finance as shares have to be made more attractive to investors to compete with interest-bearing bank deposits. This means that the company would have to offer potential investors a higher dividend, raising the cost of any funds raised on the stock market. Differences in the tax treatment of interest and dividend payments can influence the choice of finance to a company, but the overall cost is still influenced by the level of interest rates.

Clearly, as interest rates in the economy rise, the number of projects which beat the cost of finance falls. An increase in interest rates, all things being equal, will result in a fall in the number of profitable projects and a decline in investment. This can be seen from the point of view of the firm's owners who have a choice between putting money into a capital expenditure project, or investing in a risk-free government bond. The return on the latter is often referred to as the opportunity cost, as it represents the interest which would be forgone by choosing to put money into the investment project. As the opportunity cost rises, less funds will be directed into fixed investment.

As in our analysis of consumer expenditure, inflation also needs to be taken into account. The investment project will produce goods and services which will have a value in the future. If prices are expected to be significantly higher in coming years, the value of the investment increases. Thus it is the rate of interest adjusted for expected price inflation, the real rate of interest, which influences investment. This is shown in Figure 2.3, where the downward sloping line represents the number of profitable projects at each level of interest rate.

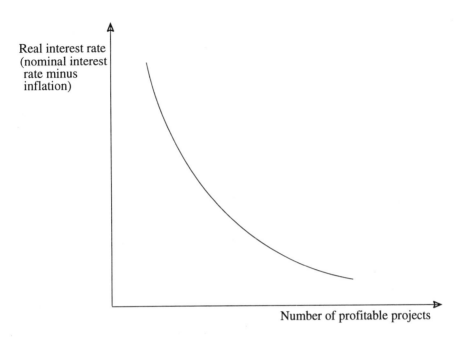

Real interest rate
(nominal interest
rate minus
inflation)

Number of profitable projects

Figure 2.3 *The investment schedule*

The availability of finance is another possible constraint on investment. If a company cannot persuade banks or the financial markets to provide funds, then its investment project is a non-starter. There has been much debate in the UK about whether small companies are being deprived of capital, but little in the way of firm conclusions. What does seem to be true, however, is that companies which are already profitable have less trouble in raising funds, and that (as we saw above) investment tends to strengthen following an economy-wide improvement in profitability.

Risk
Investment tends to suffer when the outlook for demand is uncertain. The more volatile the economic environment, the shorter the time horizons of management when planning investment; that is, the greater the risk that the demand projections could be wrong, the less chance a project has of being approved. This also applies to the cost of capital, where the owners of a company will demand that a project earns a higher premium over the cost of funds than in a stable economic environment, to compensate for the greater risk of making a loss.

We summarize the determinants of fixed investment in Table 2.4.

Table 2.4 *Key determinants of fixed investment*

Expected demand
  – economic forecasts
  – recent growth, profits
  – capacity constraints
 	
Cost of finance
  – real interest rates
 	
Risk
  – effect on demand
  – effect on cost of finance
	Fixed investment

Stockbuilding

Stockbuilding is a form of investment as it represents goods held for future delivery. Consequently it is influenced by the same factors as fixed investment, although with a shorter time horizon. As with fixed investment, changes in stockbuilding behaviour can be volatile and have a major impact on GDP.

Key Determinants

1. Expected demand
2. Cost of stockholding
3. Risk

Expected demand
Companies hold stocks to meet unforeseen changes in demand or to make up for a loss of production. In this way they can supply unexpected orders or continue to deliver if a factory goes out of operation. For a given level of output, firms will have a level of stocks which meet these needs based on past experience of fluctuations in demand and the likelihood of a loss of production. Thus the level of stocks can be expected to rise in proportion with output.

If demand rises unexpectedly, firms will initially run stocks down rather than immediately increase production. If demand then falls back, the shortfall in stocks can be made up by increasing production for a period. Only if the rise in demand proves to be permanent need the company incur the costs of adjusting production, such as taking on more workers and investing in new equipment.

In this way stocks tend to act as a buffer, while firms judge whether a change in demand is temporary or permanent. These expectations obviously then have a crucial impact on output as firms decide whether they need to make permanent changes to their production. The factors which influence firms expectations are similar to those mentioned above — current GDP growth, capacity and profits. In recent years, the level of stocks has been influenced by changes in technology, such as computerized stock control and just-in-time methods, which have resulted in a steady decline in the ratio of stocks to output.

Cost of stockholding

In choosing to hold an extra unit of output in stocks, the company will forgo the revenue which could have been obtained from selling it. The cost to the firm is the interest which could have been earned on this revenue during the period the good was held in stock. This is an opportunity cost, as it is a cost of forgoing something, rather than a pecuniary cost (such as the wage bill) which has to be paid. When interest rates rise, the opportunity cost of stockholding increases and firms have a strong incentive to cut their stocks.

Against this the firm must consider the rate of inflation. The value of a given level of stock appreciates with the price level. If prices are expected to rise rapidly over the next 12 months, a firm will have a strong incentive to hold stock and sell it for a higher price in a year's time. Conversely, if prices are expected to fall, the firm will be trying to sell its stock now. Thus, it is the real interest rate (nominal interest minus inflation) which influences the level of stocks in the economy.

Risk

In an economy where demand is very volatile, the ratio of stocks to output is likely to be greater than in a more stable environment, as there is a higher probability of a sharp increase in demand leaving companies without stocks.

These ideas can be summarized in Table 2.5.

Table 2.5   *Key determinants of stockbuilding*

Expected demand	
Cost of stockholding – real interest rates	Stockbuilding
Risk – volatility of demand	

Trade: Imports and Exports

So far we have considered demand without distinguishing whether expenditure is on domestically produced or imported goods. Clearly, higher demand will not boost domestic output if it is spent on goods produced overseas, so imports need to be deducted from domestic demand. For the same reason, we need to add back overseas demand for UK goods — exports — to determine national output, GDP.

Imports

> ### Key determinants
>
> 1. Domestic demand
> 2. Competitiveness

Domestic Demand

Imports are largely influenced by the strength of domestic demand: the stronger consumption and investment, the higher the level of imports. The composition of demand is also important. Some components of demand are more import intensive than others, reflecting the availability of domestic substitutes. In the UK, capital expenditure is import intensive as there are few domestic producers, or those firms which exist are geared to overseas markets. By contrast, a greater proportion of Germany's capital expenditure needs are met by domestic producers. Stockbuilding also tends to be import intensive in the UK, as raw materials and other commodities may not be available at home. Consumer spending is less import intensive as it includes goods which are less readily traded, such as haircuts, garage repairs and other services.

Competitiveness

If overseas goods are better value than domestic, they will be preferred. The relative price is important and this will be influenced by the exchange rate and relative inflation rates. For example, a fall in the pound makes goods produced overseas relatively more expensive when the foreign currency price is translated into sterling. UK consumers may then choose to buy more home-produced goods rather than imports from abroad. In the absence of exchange rate changes, countries with low price inflation will gain price competitiveness over those with higher inflation. That is, if UK inflation is higher than overseas, domestic goods will steadily become more expensive relative to imports, resulting in a steady rise in imports as a share of domestic demand.

Sometimes differences in competitiveness may not be reflected in price, but in quality. Consumers may prefer German motor cars, Swedish fridges and Italian suits to their UK counterparts, even if the latter are cheaper. Such non-price factors have become increasingly important in international trade, limiting the effect of a change in the exchange rate on imports.

Table 2.6 *The key determinants of imports*

Domestic demand
  – strength
  – composition
 	
Competitiveness
  – relative price
    (exchange rate, inflation)
  – relative quality
    (design, reliability)
	Imports

Exports

One country's imports are another's exports, so this section is very much the mirror image of the last.

Key Determinants

1. World demand
2. Competitiveness

World demand

World demand is the driving force behind exports. If global activity is expanding and countries are dismantling barriers to trade, then exports should grow briskly.

A country's share of world trade can be expected to increase if domestic demand is rising most rapidly in its principal trading partners. For example, the Netherlands, Belgium and France enjoyed substantial trade growth following the massive boost from German demand following the latter's reunification in 1989. In the mid-1980s exporters to North America performed well as US demand grew rapidly. Figure 2.4 shows the importance of different regions for UK exports.

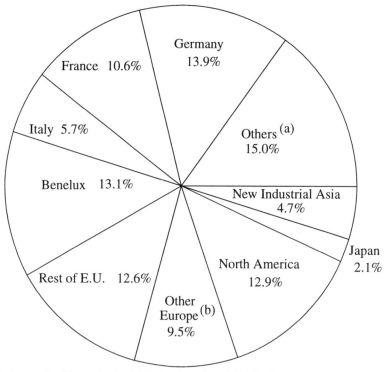

(a) Australia, New Zealand, Latin America, Middle East & N. Africa, S. Africa and India.

(b) Norway, Sweden, Switzerland, Finland, Austria, Iceland, former Soviet Union and E.Europe.

Source: Monthly Review of External Trade Statistics.

Figure 2.4   *UK exports by destination, % of total*

Competitiveness

A lack of competitiveness will limit a country's share of world trade. The same factors which influence imports apply here. Countries with relatively high inflation are likely to suffer a steady erosion of their share of world trade as their goods become progressively more expensive. Only if the increase in their export prices is offset by a fall in the value of their currency will they be able to maintain price competitiveness. Non-price factors such as design, service and reliability are also important in determining a country's share of world trade.

Table 2.7 *The key influences on exports*

World demand
  – strength
  – composition
 	
Competitiveness
  – relative price
  – relative quality
	Exports

Dynamics

In practice the elements of aggregate demand are interrelated. The economy is dynamic, with changes in one sector feeding into other sectors. For example, an increase in consumers' expenditure will increase the output of firms producing consumer goods, who in turn may decide to order more capital equipment, thus boosting investment. This in turn may lead to an increase in employment and higher consumer incomes, which feed back into stronger consumer spending. These interactions are important, but we have discussed each component separately so as to focus on the key determinants of each. This then enables us to isolate the key forces in the economy, be they rising house prices and consumer spending, or strong overseas demand and increasing exports.

Summary

1. Gross Domestic Product (GDP) is the value of goods and services produced by the economy. It is expressed in real terms by adjusting for price increases to leave the volume of production.

2. GDP can be measured by either adding up the goods and services produced by each sector in the economy (output approach), summing wages and profits (the income method), or totalling the expenditure of those who purchase finished goods and services (the expenditure approach).

3. Because the value of output produced equals the value of sales, which in turn is equivalent to the wages and profits of the economy, the three approaches should all produce the same outcome for GDP.

4. The analysis of GDP from the demand side is based on the expenditure components of GDP — consumers' expenditure, fixed investment and stockbuilding, government consumption and imports and exports.

5. Consumers' expenditure represents spending by the personal sector on goods and services and is the largest component of GDP. It is determined by real income, asset prices and real interest rates.

6. Government consumption represents goods and services provided by the government but mainly paid for out of taxation rather than direct charges. It includes health, education and defence.

7. Investment, in both fixed capacity and stocks, is the most volatile component of GDP. Fixed investment represents expenditure on plant and equipment, housing, roads and other infrastructure projects and is carried out by both the private and public sectors. It is determined by the expected level of demand and real interest rates. Stocks are influenced by the same factors, but with a shorter time horizon. They tend to be higher if demand is volatile as there is a greater risk of running short of stock.

8. Imports are goods and services bought by domestic residents but made abroad, and therefore need to be deducted from domestic expenditure in the calculation of GDP. They are determined by the strength and composition of domestic demand and their competitiveness relative to domestic substitutes.

9. Exports are goods and services made at home but sold overseas and therefore need to be included in the calculation of GDP. They are determined by the strength and composition of world demand and their competitiveness in international markets.

Questions for consideration

1. How would an increase in interest rates affect GDP? Trace out the effects through each component of expenditure.
2. Savings are often seen as a 'good thing' and governments have been known to exhort people to save more. Using the demand framework of this chapter, how would an increase in saving affect GDP?
3. A fall in the exchange rate should improve competitiveness. Why? How will this affect GDP if there are no domestic substitutes for imports, while exports face no competition overseas?
4. How might an increase in fixed investment in the US affect UK GDP?
5. Consider the products produced by your firm or one you know well. Which category of expenditure do they fall under? How important are the key determinants described above for their markets?

Further reading

For further details of the measurement of GDP see *UK National Accounts — Sources and methods*, Central Statistical Office (CSO). The latest figures for the UK can be found in *Economic Trends* (published monthly by the CSO), or the *UK National Accounts* ('The Blue Book', published annually by the CSO).

For the latest thinking on consumer spending see 'Consumption' (*Oxford Review of Economic Policy*, Summer 1994) and 'Housing, Consumption and Borrowing: An assessment of recent personal sector behaviour in the UK' (*National Institute Economic Review*, 3, 1994). On investment see *The Investment Decisions of Firms*, S Nickell (Oxford University Press, 1978). UK trade performance is examined in 'Is the UK Balance of Payments Sustainable', J Muellbauer and A Murphy (*Economic Policy*, October 1990) and *The State of the Economy* (Institute for Economic Affairs, 1990).

Inflation

Inflation has been described as the scourge of the modern economy, and a low and stable inflation rate has become the principal, sometimes the sole objective of economic policy in nearly all the major economies.

The aims of this chapter are:

1. to show what inflation is and why it is a problem;
2. to describe the determinants of inflation;
3. to explain cycles in growth and inflation.

What is inflation?

The rate of inflation is the percentage increase in the general level of prices in a given period. It is normally measured by taking the change in a price index which captures the prices of a broad range of goods (such as the Retail Price Index in the UK) over a period of a year. Inflation has two key features.

First, it is a continuous rather than a one-off process. Inflation occurs where prices are being marked up on a regular basis. In contrast, if prices double overnight but then remain stable, there would not be an inflation problem.

Second, inflation is an increase in the general level of prices rather than an increase in the price of a specific good. We need to distinguish between general inflation and the changes in relative prices which occur in any market economy. For example, food prices may be rising but this could be offset by declines in the prices of computers and videos. While this may have important social consequences, it is a change in relative rather than general prices and so in principle is not inflation.

Costs of inflation

If prices are rising, purchasing power is being steadily eroded. Figure 3.1 shows that one pound in 1960 is now worth less than 10p — ie £1 in 1960 could buy more than 10 times as many goods and services as it can today. This has the effect of redistributing income

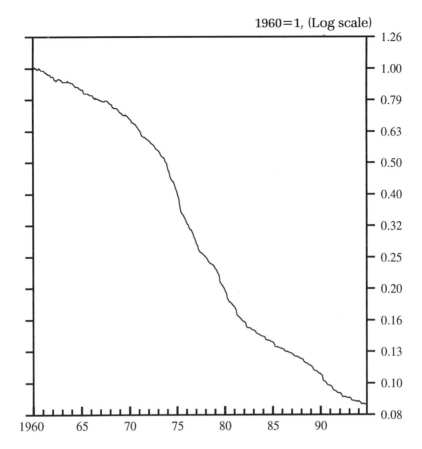

1960=1, (Log scale)

Source: CSO, authors' own calculations based on Retail Price Index

Figure 3.1 *The declining purchasing power of the pound*

from creditors to debtors, and from those on fixed incomes to those in work. For example, the tenfold increase in the price level since 1960 means that those who had borrowed in 1960 saw their debt reduced by 90 per cent in real terms, while those who had saved experienced a similar reduction in the real value of their investment. Those on fixed incomes were particularly badly hit as their incomes dwindled in real terms; those in work were less affected as pay increases more than compensated for the rise in prices. These effects have clearly been inequitable and have tended to encourage people to borrow rather than save.

However, most of these costs arose because the inflation was unanticipated. They could have been avoided if contracts, such as pensions, had been adjusted for inflation, while the real value of savings could have been preserved if the government had kept interest rates above inflation. Since the 1970s, linking contracts to inflation has become more widespread and the government has recognized the importance of keeping real interest rates positive. However, even when households and firms have made arrangements to insulate themselves from inflation it can still impose costs on an economy.

Inflation creates uncertainty. The higher the inflation rate the more variable it tends to be, and this makes future prices less predictable. In this uncertain environment, investment tends to suffer as businesses find it harder to calculate the prices they will receive in the future, and therefore the expected returns on a project.

For similar reasons, lenders will demand a greater real return when inflation is high to compensate for the risk of inflation accelerating. This effect can be seen in financial markets where governments with a poor inflation record have to pay a significant premium in interest over their inflation rate, compared with low inflation countries.

Finally, rising inflation can have an impact on the competitiveness of an economy. If prices are rising faster at home than overseas, the economy is gradually losing competitiveness as its goods and services are becoming more and more expensive relative to those made abroad. As mentioned in Chapter 2, this will tend to result in a declining share of world trade, with exports weaker and imports stronger than they would have been otherwise. In principle this loss of competitiveness can be offset by a depreciation in the exchange rate. This has been the route followed by the UK, where sterling has been persistently devalued to offset higher inflation. Currency depreciation has enabled the UK to maintain competitiveness, but has also allowed policy-makers to avoid tackling the underlying sources of inflation.

The combined effect of these factors is to depress GDP growth. Weaker investment, higher borrowing costs and a persistent loss of competitiveness all weigh on activity. Recent research indicates that countries with low inflation tend to enjoy higher productivity. It is for these reasons that a low and stable rate of inflation has become the principal objective of economic policy among the industrialized economies. We now turn to the underlying causes of inflation.

Determinants of inflation

What causes inflation to rise?

When the demand for goods and services exceeds the supply, prices rise more rapidly. This applies as much to the macroeconomy as it does to individual markets. If the economy is operating close to its physical limits, firms will be unable to meet an increase in demand by increasing output and instead will raise their prices more quickly. If demand remains above supply, inflation will accelerate. Conversely, when demand is below supply, prices are subdued and inflation decelerates.

We take a detailed look at these processes below, but first we need to consider the factors which influence the economy's ability to supply goods and services. This is often referred to as *aggregate supply*, as we are considering the whole economy rather than an individual sector.

Determinants of aggregate supply

Resources
The amount the economy can supply (often known as productive potential) depends on the labour available, the capital stock and an element called *total factor productivity* (TFP), which represents the efficiency with which capital and labour are combined. Thus, TFP is a 'catch-all' term for the effects on production of technological progress, better management and improved education. Two economies with the same resources of labour and capital can produce different amounts if total factor productivity is higher in one than the other.

Production function
To determine the growth in supply it is first necessary to specify how output relates to the inputs of capital and labour. This is called a *production function* and economists normally make the simplifying assumption that a 1 per cent increase in labour and capital results in a 1 per cent rise in production, known as *constant returns to scale*. The growth in output which cannot be accounted for by the increase in labour and capital is then attributed to total factor productivity. For example, if inputs of labour and capital rise by 1 per cent and output rises by 2 per cent, total factor productivity growth is 1 per cent.

Estimating supply
To project supply we then need to estimate the likely growth in labour and capital. The labour input will be directly related to population growth, participation rates (workers per capita) and changes to the length of the working week. Thus the estimate needs to take into account population demographics and trends such as the increasing participation of women in the workforce, and shorter working hours.

Estimates of the likely growth in the capital stock can be based on the rise in fixed capital investment relative to the depreciation (ie wear and tear) of the existing stock of plant, equipment, offices and buildings. The capital stock will rise if new investment exceeds depreciation. Total factor productivity is normally projected forward from recent history as the influence of technology, better management and education is assumed to be gradual. We show a calculation of aggregate supply for the UK below.

Estimating aggregate supply for the UK

In the Bank of England model of the UK economy, the growth in supply is described by the following production function

$$\text{GDP (supply)} = 0.7^*L + 0.3^*K + T$$

where L is the growth in the labour force, K is the growth in the capital stock and T is total factor productivity (assumed to be a constant adding 1.25 per cent to supply each year). Thus, if the labour force and capital stock increase by 1 per cent per year, potential supply will rise by 2.25 per cent (calculated as $0.7^*1.0 + 0.3^*1.0 + 1.25$).

Using government projections of the growth in the labour force and estimates of the increase in capital stock, we can use the above equation to project supply.

Projection of supply (percentage change, year on year)

Year	Labour force	Capital stock	TFP	Aggregate supply
1995	0.4	3.1	1.25	2.4
1996	0.4	2.8	1.25	2.4
1997	0.6	2.9	1.25	2.5
1998	0.5	2.7	1.25	2.4
1999	0.4	2.8	1.25	2.4

This then gives us a central projection for aggregate supply growth of 2.4 per cent per year in the five years to 1999. With the labour force rising by about 0.5 per cent per year, this represents an increase in productivity (output per worker) of 2 per cent per year.

Potential output and inflation

The central projection of supply, based on the resources available to the economy, is known as *potential output*. When the economy is at potential, firms are operating at normal levels of output and labour is available to meet the increase in demand. Consequently, inflation is stable. When GDP rises above potential, the economy's resources come under strain and inflation accelerates. Increased pressure on prices comes from two sources.

First, labour costs rise. Increasing overtime and recruiting extra workers from the pool of unemployed enable the economy to raise its output above potential. However, overtime is paid at premium rates and, if firms bid for outside labour, wage rates generally will rise as companies compete for scarce skills. Wages account for over two-thirds of the economy's costs (based on the income estimate of GDP, see Chapter 2), and so higher labour charges substantially increase the cost of production. Many companies set their prices as a mark-up on costs, and consequently higher labour costs are passed on to the customer in the form of higher prices. Figure 3.2 shows the close correlation between unit labour costs (the total wage bill divided by output) and inflation in the UK (shown here as the annual change in the Retail Price Index).

Secondly, in addition to the first effect, firms will take advantage of the strength of demand to increase the mark-up over costs, ie expand their profit margins. This effect becomes increasingly important as companies approach the limits of their production. If the firm cannot increase production without making a major investment in plant and machinery, or if there are simply no spare workers available, it will offer the same amount of goods at a higher price.

Therefore, from a combination of having to cover higher labour costs and increasing their mark-up, firms raise their prices more rapidly when the economy goes above potential. Inflation accelerates.

When the economy goes below potential these factors go into reverse. The costs of production fall as overtime is cut back and, as unemployment increases and people compete for work, there is downward pressure on wages. Firms are also likely to trim their profit margins as they try to utilize their spare plant and equipment which has been made idle by the fall in demand. Therefore, through a combination of lower unit labour costs and a narrowing of profit margins, inflation decelerates when activity is below potential.

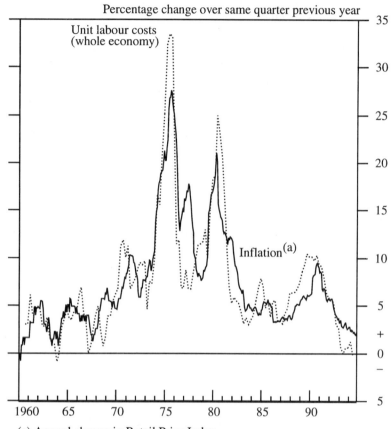

Percentage change over same quarter previous year

(a) Annual change in Retail Price Index.

Source: CSO

Figure 3.2   *Unit labour costs and inflation*

Output gap

The difference between actual and potential GDP is known as the
output gap. When GDP is above potential the economy is said to have
a positive output gap, and when GDP is below potential, a negative
output gap. Inflation will be rising when the output gap is positive
and falling when the gap is negative. This means, however, that
there is no simple stable relationship between inflation and growth:
if real GDP is rising, inflation could be rising or falling (we look at the
growth/inflation cycle later in this chapter). Nevertheless, there is a
trade-off, at least in the short run, between inflation and unemployment. To see this we need to focus on the links between the labour
market and wage inflation.

Labour market

Phillips curve
Clearly the labour market is very important as a transmitter of inflation, and this analysis is often described in terms of unemployment
rather than supply or potential output. When unemployment is high
there is downward pressure on wages and consequently inflation
decelerates. Conversely, when unemployment is low, wages and
inflation accelerate. In the past it was believed that there was a stable trade-off between unemployment and wage growth, so
policy-makers could choose between different combinations of
growth and inflation. The relationship between wages and unemployment was called the *Phillips curve* (after the economist who
originally described it) and is shown in Figure 3.3. For example,
wages might be rising at 3 per cent per year when unemployment
was equal to 6 per cent of the workforce, but would rise at 5 per cent
if unemployment fell to 4 per cent.

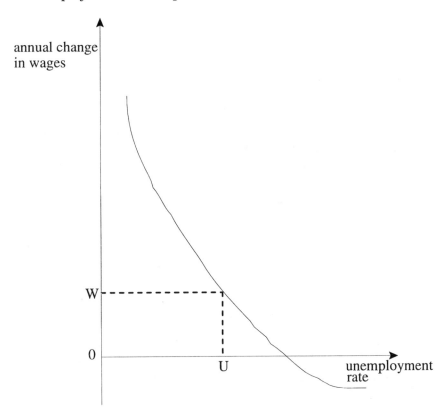

Figure 3.3 *The Phillips curve*

Natural rate of unemployment

Over the past 20 years the Phillips curve relationship has broken down. Unemployment has had to rise higher and higher to stabilize inflation, and there has been no stable trade-off between the two.

The reason for this is that workers' wage demands are also influenced by their expectations of inflation as well as unemployment. Therefore, if workers expected inflation to accelerate, wage demands would rise without any change in unemployment. The Phillips curve would move upward and the trade-off between unemployment and inflation would worsen.

These arguments were developed further by Milton Friedman who argued that there was a natural rate of unemployment at which the Phillips curve was vertical, ie in the long run there was no trade-off between unemployment and inflation. If the government stimulated growth and reduced unemployment, inflation would rise as the economy moved along its Phillips curve. This would then prompt an increase in wage demands which would cause inflation to accelerate further. This process would continue, with the Phillips curve continuously shifting up as wages and prices chased each other. The spiral could only be broken if the government allowed demand to fall back, and unemployment to return to its natural rate.

The idea of a natural rate of unemployment, at which wages and inflation are stable, is widely accepted. The natural rate, sometimes known as the *non-accelerating inflation rate of unemployment* (the NAIRU), is determined by the characteristics of the labour market, such as the wage bargaining system, the level of social security benefit and the average duration of unemployment. Depending on these factors, the natural rate can change over time. The more flexible the labour market, ie the more quickly and easily the unemployed find new jobs, the lower the natural rate of unemployment. The breakdown in the relationship between inflation and unemployment is now attributed to a rising natural rate of unemployment. In the UK, for example, the natural rate of unemployment is currently thought to be around 8 per cent. Thirty years ago inflation was stable with unemployment at around 3 per cent. We look at the determinants of the natural rate in more detail in Chapter 8.

Natural rate of unemployment and potential output

In terms of our earlier analysis the economy is at its potential when unemployment is at its natural rate. If unemployment rises above its natural rate, there is downward pressure on labour costs and inflation falls. Conversely, if unemployment is below its natural rate there is upward pressure on wage costs and inflation rises.

Table 3.1   *Output, unemployment and inflation*

Output (GDP)	Unemployment	Inflation
Above potential	Below natural rate	Rising
At potential	At natural rate	Stable
Below potential	Above natural rate	Falling

Inflation in the long run

Our analysis so far has concentrated on the dynamics of inflation, why inflation rises or falls. However, we have not answered the question of what determines the rate of inflation in the long run when activity has returned to potential and unemployment is at its natural rate. That is, at what level does inflation stabilize?

Price expectations

One factor we have already mentioned in our discussion of the Phillips curve is the influence of expected inflation on wage bargaining. The level that wage expectations settle at when the labour market is at its natural rate will depend on people's perception of 'normal' inflation. This in turn will primarily depend on the country's inflation history and the extent to which government intentions to reduce inflation are believed. Countries with a record of low inflation and credible anti-inflationary policies will have a lower equilibrium inflation rate than those without these attributes. We look at these factors and the role they play in government policy in Chapter 5.

Money growth

The second factor which determines the rate of inflation in the long run is the growth in the money supply: the ultimate cause of inflation is 'too much money chasing too few goods'. This follows from the *quantity equation*, which describes the relationship between the value of production and the money stock:

$$M.V = P.T$$

where M = the money stock
V = the velocity of circulation, the number of times the money stock circulates in a given period
P = the general price level
T = the number of transactions, the real GDP of the economy

This equation is known as an identity because it is true by definition. It simply states that the total money value of transactions in a given period (the stock of money multiplied by the number of times it has circulated through the economy, MV) is equal to the total money value of goods and services sold (the number of transactions times the general price level, PT).

On the assumption that the velocity of circulation is stable, changes in money growth will be reflected in changes in nominal GDP. For example, if the money stock is rising at 5 per cent per annum (pa) then GDP growth plus inflation must equal 5 per cent pa. Over the long term GDP will rise in line with its trend, say 3 per cent pa, implying an inflation rate of 2 per cent pa. This would be the prevailing inflation rate in the economy when activity was at potential. The quantity equation implies that the authorities can determine inflation by controlling the money supply, and we look at this in more detail in Chapter 5.

Policy errors and supply-side shocks

If the economy could be kept at its trend and money growth under control, inflation would be stable. Therefore, it is the factors which can drive the economy away from its potential, or cause the government to lose control of the money supply, which actually cause fluctuations in inflation. In general these are of two sorts.

Policy errors
It is often difficult to judge where the economy is in relation to its trend. Economic data is released with a lag and changes in policy take time to affect the economy. Moreover, political pressures may cause a government to take the view that unemployment is above its natural rate, when in reality it is below and a recession is needed to get inflation under control. Either way, inappropriate attempts by governments to stimulate demand have been responsible for fluctuations in inflation. Similar pressures may account for the authorities' loss of control of the money supply and the subsequent rise in inflation.

Supply-side shocks
Even when there is agreement on where the economy is in its growth cycle, a shock, such as a rise in oil prices, may trigger an acceleration in inflation. A sharp increase in costs will push up prices, but it can develop into sustained inflation if higher prices are allowed to feed into wages. The workforce will demand an increase in wages to compensate for the fall in their standard of living. If achieved this will push companies' costs up further and lead to a

second round of price increases. In this way inflation accelerates as prices and costs chase each other upwards.

Clearly, if unemployment is above its natural rate when the shock occurs there will already be downward pressure on pay settlements and a wage-price spiral is less likely to develop. However, in the case of an oil shock the situation is complicated as the increase in costs renders some energy-intensive plant and machinery obsolete. Previously profitable operations go out of business, plant and machinery are scrapped and the economy's potential output is reduced. The economy is less able to supply goods and services and so price pressures increase.

If activity had previously been at potential, it is now below it and inflation will begin to rise. The economy must now experience a fall in GDP to return it to potential; or, to put this another way, the level of unemployment, which had previously been sufficient to keep inflation stable, needs to rise. It is often policy-makers' reluctance to acknowledge the harsh reality of this which leads to higher wages and accelerating inflation.

To prevent inflation the government needs to meet the initial increase in prices with a tough monetary and fiscal stance: demand will then fall and firms will not be able to sustain price rises. Workers may be able to achieve higher wages at first, but this will only be temporary as firms will experience a squeeze on their profit margins and will lay people off. Higher unemployment will then cause workers to moderate their pay claims, thus checking the wage-price spiral.

The Growth/Inflation cycle

In this section we draw on our analysis of actual and potential output to describe how growth and inflation behave over an economic cycle.

It is often thought that faster growth and accelerating inflation go together. In practice the two can move in opposite directions, and in this section we use the concept of potential output to describe how inflation and GDP growth behave. From this we can identify different stages of the business cycle.

Phase 1: Overheating — inflationary growth

Figure 3.4 plots the growth rate of GDP and inflation when the economy is first above, and then below, its potential. Starting at point *a*, output is rising, but with the economy above potential inflation is also increasing (the figure shows the growth rate falling and the inflation rate rising). The economy is overheating as higher demand is leading to faster inflation rather than growth.

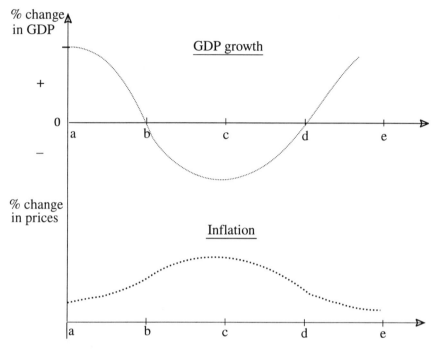

Between points *a* and *c* the economy is above potential, and between *c* and *e* it is below potential.

Figure 3.4   *GDP growth and inflation*

Phase 2: Recession — stagflation

At point *b*, output stops rising and begins to fall. The economy is in recession. However, between *b* and *c*, GDP is still above potential so inflation continues to rise. This combination of falling output and rising inflation is known as *stagflation*.

Phase 3: Recession — deflation

At point *c*, GDP falls below potential and inflation begins to fall. The economy is still in recession as GDP is still falling, but inflation is now declining.

Phase 4: Recovery — non-inflationary growth

At point *d* output stops falling and begins to recover. Between points *d* and *e*, rising GDP is accompanied by falling inflation, a golden combination which often creates the impression that inflation is no longer a problem. Instead it simply reflects the fact that the economy is below potential and there are spare resources available to meet rising demand.

The UK experience 1978-94

The recession of 1980–81 took actual GDP almost 5 per cent below its potential. Consequently, as activity recovered inflation continued to fall, until 1986 when the gap with potential was closed. After 1986, GDP continued to rise strongly and went significantly above potential. As a result inflation rose sharply. In 1990 activity slowed and the economy went into recession. However, as GDP was still above potential, inflation continued to rise and the economy entered a period of stagflation. By 1991 GDP had fallen below its potential and inflation began to fall sharply. In 1992 activity began to recover, but as GDP was below potential, inflation continued to fall.

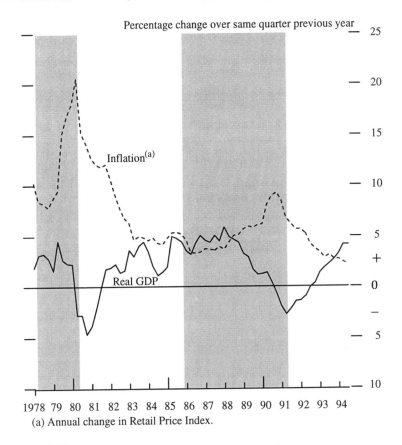

Percentage change over same quarter previous year

(a) Annual change in Retail Price Index.

Source: CSO

Shaded areas are periods when the economy is above its potential.

Figure 3.5   *UK growth and inflation 1978–94*

Balance of Payments: the inflation safety valve

This framework can also be used to analyse a country's *balance of payments*, the difference between exports and imports. If an economy demands more than it produces, it has to import the extra goods and services from abroad. In terms of the expenditure components of national output, the economy has a balance of payments deficit when domestic demand is greater than GDP (ie imports exceed exports). Thus the balance of payments deficit can be thought of as the gap between domestic demand and actual GDP. If we add domestic demand to our model of actual and potential output, we can track the trade deficit as well as inflation.

The balance of payments can be expected to deteriorate as activity rises above potential, and domestic producers become increasingly capacity constrained. In these circumstances domestic consumers will turn to overseas suppliers to meet their needs and imports will rise sharply. Unless there is an offsetting rise from exports, the balance of payments will deteriorate. In this way imports act as a safety valve for the economy, as they take the pressure off domestic producers by diverting demand overseas. Without this outlet inflation would be higher, as domestic producers would try to choke off the excess demand by raising their prices more rapidly. Nevertheless, a deterioration in the balance of payments owing to a sharp rise in imports is often a signal that activity is above its potential and that inflation is about to rise.

Summary

1. Inflation is the percentage increase in the general level of prices in a given period (usually one year).

2. Inflation redistributes income from creditors to debtors and from those on fixed incomes to those in work. Even when these effects are anticipated, inflation imposes costs on the economy by increasing uncertainty.

3. Fluctuations in inflation reflect an imbalance between supply and demand in the economy.

4. The amount an economy can supply will depend on its resources of labour and capital, and the efficiency with which they are combined. Supply rises steadily over time and is known as the economy's potential output.

5. When an increase in demand takes output above potential, labour costs rise and profit margins expand, thus pushing up prices faster than before — inflation accelerates. Conversely, when output goes below potential, inflation decelerates.

6. The level of unemployment influences inflation through its effect on wages. Unemployment is said to be at its natural rate when wage growth and inflation are stable. By definition, the economy is at potential when unemployment is at its natural rate.

7. In the long run, activity will move in line with its potential, and the inflation rate is determined by inflationary expectations and the growth in the money supply.

8. Errors of demand management and supply-side shocks have been responsible for fluctuations in inflation, by causing actual demand to differ from supply.

9. The behaviour of GDP growth and inflation can be described using the model of actual and potential output. This enables us to identify the different stages of the business cycle — overheating, recession and recovery.

10. The current account of the balance of payments acts as a safety valve for inflation by diverting excess demand overseas and preventing the economy from rising further above potential.

Questions for consideration

1. How would an increase in commodity prices affect inflation? Consider the effect on the costs of production and distinguish between whether the economy is above or below potential.

2. People in Germany consider an inflation rate of 5 per cent to be high. How does this make it easier to control inflation? (*Hint*: think about wage bargaining.)

3. How does increased competition from the Far East affect inflation in the major industrialized economies? (Think about the direct effect on prices and the indirect influences on wages.)

4. Look at the pricing behaviour of your organization. How closely does it correspond to the description contained in this chapter? Is there a level of activity at which prices in your industry begin to accelerate?

Further reading

For a good history of inflation in the UK see 'Inflation over 300 years' (*Bank of England Quarterly Bulletin*, May 1994). The costs and causes of inflation are looked at in detail in 'Inflation' (*Oxford Review of Economic Policy*, Winter 1990), and in a chapter on the labour market in *The Performance of the British Economy* (R Dornbusch and R Layard (eds), Oxford University Press, 1987).

4

Fiscal policy

The aims of this chapter are to show you:

1. the principles underlying government spending and taxation;
2. how to predict the impact of changes in fiscal policy on the economy;
3. how to evaluate the influence of government finances on future fiscal policy and the economy.

Once a year the government announces its fiscal policy in the form of the Budget. In judging what measures to announce, the government must take into account many competing claims. Although a number of political aims may influence the Budget judgement, there are two main economic considerations:

1. *How much government should spend.* This decision has two parts: a microeconomic choice of what areas of economic activity the government should be involved in; and a macroeconomic choice of what effect changes in government spending will have on aggregate output and inflation.
2. *How this spending should be financed.* Governments can choose between tax revenue and borrowing as ways of financing a given level of spending. These two forms of financing have different effects on the economy and the government can also use this choice to achieve its macroeconomic aims.

The decisions that the government makes over fiscal policy can have important implications for business. Business can be directly affected by changes in taxes and subsidies, or indirectly affected by the impact of fiscal policy on overall demand. These effects mean that it is important for firms to be able to predict when the stance of fiscal policy is likely to be changed. For example, what causes governments to ignore large budget deficits in some circumstances and not in others? Businesses also need to understand what effect a change in fiscal policy is likely to have on aggregate demand.

Government Spending and Taxation

The most important way in which fiscal policy can affect individuals and firms is through how spending is allocated. For example, regional grants can dramatically change the economic climate in the areas which receive them. Although decisions about individual government projects are made on a case-by-case basis, there are some general principles used to guide fiscal policy which can help outside observers to guess which projects are likely to be undertaken. This section outlines some of those principles.

Government spending is a large and growing part of total spending in most countries. However, most governments profess to support the free market as the best and most efficient way of allocating resources. This apparent contradiction is not simply political doubletalk and can often be justified on economic grounds. For instance, although the market is more efficient in most circumstances, it sometimes delivers results that are politically or socially undesirable. It can also in some cases be less efficient. Governments therefore usually elect to override free market allocation in the areas of public goods and natural monopolies.

Public goods are goods which benefit others as well the direct purchaser. National defence is a classic example of a public good, because an individual's contribution to the cost of the armed forces of a country is clearly of benefit to everyone, not just to the individual. The problem with a market allocation of public goods is the 'free rider'; that is, anyone invited to purchase a public good may decline to do so in the hope that he or she will be able to get a free ride or benefit from some other person's purchase. The government therefore may have to step in to make sure that enough of the public good is produced or purchased.

The free market may also lead to inefficient outcomes in the case of natural monopolies. A *natural monopoly* is an industry in which it is most efficient for a single producer to operate. Such natural monopolies include the telephone system and electricity distribution. In the case of the latter, competition could only be introduced into the market by duplicating electricity supply cables. The enormous extra capital cost would probably make this solution less efficient than that of a single operator. Of course, the single operator may try to exploit its monopoly power by overcharging for its services. Many countries have attempted to solve this problem by bringing the monopoly producer under government control, although the alternative of privatizing the monopoly and then regulating it (eg OFTEL and OFGAS) is becoming increasingly popular.

Of course, government spending is not only directed at overcoming market inefficiencies. Governments also have political and social aims and usually decide that free market allocation in certain cases is unfair. Such cases include education, health care, pensions and a basic income during unemployment.

Taxation

In principle, a tax system should aim to finance public expenditure with the minimum possible distortion of the economic decisions of the rest of the economy; this principle is called *fiscal neutrality*. In order to achieve fiscal neutrality, taxation must be balanced across different markets so that it minimizes the tendency for people or firms to base economic decisions on tax avoidance.

Despite growing support for this idea, governments' success in implementing fiscal neutrality has been limited. This is partly because, as we saw above, governments accept that some distortion is desirable if it helps to avoid extremes of poverty and wealth. Most governments therefore aim to make the tax system *progressive* — ie richer people pay a higher proportion of their income in tax than poorer people. There are other reasons why fiscal neutrality is rarely achieved in practice. For instance, the tax system may fail to deliver this objective simply because the implications of a particular tax are not properly understood, or because a distortionary tax is easier to implement and collect than a fiscally neutral one.

Governments must also consider the effects of taxation on people's incentive to work. Two opposite effects can be identified. The first, called the *income effect*, causes people to work more because taxation reduces their income level and they seek to restore it. The second, called the *substitution effect*, results from a lower net monetary return from working and induces people to work less hard — leisure time is therefore substituted for working time.

Which of these effects is more important in practice? Professor Laffer (an economic adviser to former US President Reagan) argued that as the tax rate increased the substitution effect would increase (obviously, in the extreme case with tax rates at 100 per cent no one would work at all). This notion formed the basis of the Laffer curve, shown in Figure 4.1, which illustrates potential tax revenue from different tax rates. An increase in the tax rate will tend to increase revenue, but as tax rates get very high, the reduced incentive to work and the increased incentive to evade tax mean that revenue begins to fall. The Laffer curve demonstrates that at very high rates of tax a decrease in the overall tax rate can actually increase tax revenue by encouraging people to work harder (the substitution effect) and spend less effort on avoiding tax, thereby increasing the amount of tax actually paid.

An important consideration in setting fiscal policy is deciding whereabouts on the Laffer curve the economy actually is. Some of President Reagan's advisers in the mid-1980s argued that the US economy was in the downward sloping part of the Laffer curve and so a decrease in tax rates would actually increase tax revenue. They were proved wrong, and the US budget deficit increased sharply.

Macroeconomic Effects of Fiscal Policy

So far this chapter has looked at how fiscal policy can be used to achieve microeconomic objectives. Governments can also use fiscal policy to adjust aggregate demand and keep the economy growing steadily. For example, in a recession the government may decide to reduce taxes and/or increase spending to stimulate demand and so

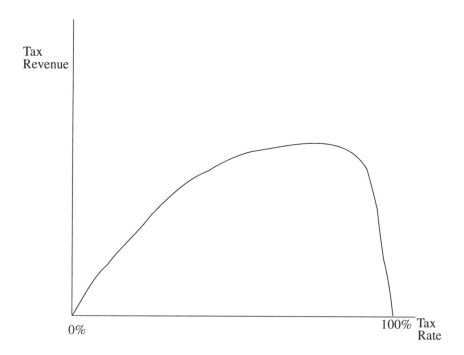

Figure 4.1   *The Laffer curve*

bring demand back to potential. Of course, the macroeconomic objectives of stabilizing the economy need not coincide with the microeconomic objectives of fiscal policy. In fact, many economists believe that too much emphasis has been put on macroeconomic objectives, or 'fine tuning' as they call it, rather than on microeconomic objectives such as fiscal neutrality.

What effect does fiscal policy have on aggregate demand?

When governments announce an increase in government spending or a change in taxation, it is important for businesses to have some idea what effect such a policy could have. For example, how much effect will a tax cut have on demand? How long will it take to feed through to the rest of the economy?

One might think that a £100 million increase in government spending would increase aggregate demand by the same amount. Although this sounds sensible, it is wrong. If the government increases public spending by, say, £100 million, the impact on aggregate demand could in fact be far greater than £100 million. Moreover, an increase in government spending (or a reduction in taxation) will continue to boost the economy for many years after the initial fiscal action.

Increases (or decreases) in government spending have a powerful effect on demand due to the *multiplier effect*. This is produced by the additional spending that an initial increase in government spending generates. For example, if the government spends £100 million on building roads, then the owners and employees of the road-building companies will be £100 million better off than they were before. As a result, they will spend some portion of that money on other goods, making a second tranche of people better off and thereby further increasing total demand. This will lead to a third round of increased spending, and so on.

The extent of this multiplier effect is determined by three factors — people's propensity to save; their propensity to buy imported rather than home-produced goods; and the rate of tax applicable to their spending. Every round of spending that follows from the initial government expenditure is reduced by the extent to which people save, buy imports and pay tax. In this context savings, imports and tax are called *leakages* because they slowly dissipate the multiplier effect. Thus, in the example above, if we assume that the tax rate is 25 per cent and people's propensity to save and to import were both 12.5 per cent of pre-tax income (ie 12.5 per cent of an increase in income would be saved and 12.5 per cent spent on imports), then the £100 million increase in the income of the road-builders would result in an increase in expenditure on UK goods of only £50 million (since they would, in aggregate, save £12.5 million, spend £12.5 million on imports and pay £25 million in tax). In the next round, on the same assumptions, the £50 million increased UK income from the first round of spending would generate £25 million extra spending on UK goods. The process of successively smaller rounds of increased spending would continue until the spending increases became negligible. In this illustration, the total increase in demand, after all the successive rounds of spending had been completed, would be £200 million — ie twice as large as the initial extra government expenditure.

When governments change taxes the multiplier effect is smaller because, unlike extra spending, a change in taxes does not increase GDP directly. For example, people will save some proportion of a tax cut and thereby reduce its impact on GDP. Table 4.1 shows estimates from three leading UK macroeconomic models of the effect of a 1p cut in income tax on GDP. In particular, it shows how a tax change can continue affecting GDP up to five years later.

Table 4.1   *The effect of a 1 per cent tax cut on GDP*

| | Estimated % increase in GDP according to: | | |
	Treasury model	London Business School model	National Institute for Economic and Social Research model
Year 1	0.1	0.1	0.2
Year 2	0.2	0.1	0.3
Year 3	0.3	0.2	0.3
Year 4	0.4	0.3	0.3
Year 5	0.5	0.4	0.3

Source: *Warwick University Ready Reckoner,* 1993

Remember, increasing aggregate demand is not the same as increasing the long-run growth of the economy. As we saw in Chapter 3, unless an increase in actual aggregate demand is matched by an increase in potential output, it will ultimately only lead to inflation and/or a worsening of the trade balance. Ideally therefore, fiscal policy should only be used to bring aggregate

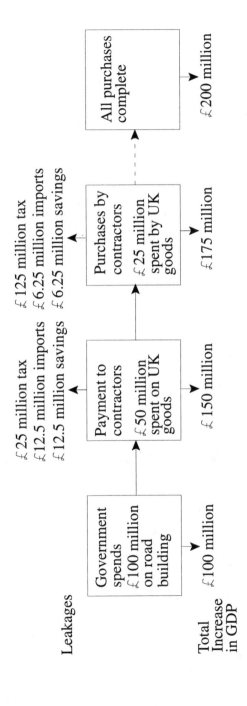

Figure 4.2 *The Multiplier process*

demand back in line with potential. Unfortunately, governments often fail to resist the temptation to stimulate aggregate demand through fiscal policy for political rather than economic reasons.

Fiscal politics

How do politics affect economic policy? Two obvious ways are through partisan effects and election cycle effects. Partisan effects on policy occur because left-wing parties prefer, on average, lower unemployment and higher inflation than do right-wing ones, so left-wing parties will tend to expand the economy and generate higher inflation and lower unemployment. Election cycles can occur because governments of any persuasion will tend to follow restrictive polices directly after being elected and then expand the economy just before an election. Election cycles are based on the idea that government's know they can maximize the chances of being re-elected if the economy is growing in the run-up to an election.

Do these two effects occur in practice? In an exhaustive study of political changes in 12 countries, Alesina conducted tests of these effects. First he looked at the average inflation, growth and unemployment in the first two years of a new political regime compared with the previous regime. He found that in about 75 per cent of cases the results fitted in with the partisan view, and that growth and inflation were higher and unemployment lower when a left-wing party was in power rather than a right-wing one. However, when he went on to look at the election cycle he found that the results were less conclusive. When testing the election cycle theory he looked exclusively at the performance of left-wing governments, reasoning that if a right-wing government had lower growth at the beginning of its term than in an election year that could well be the result of partisan effects (a right-wing government might have to have tight policies at the beginning of its term to bring inflation down to its desired level). He looked at average growth and unemployment in election year compared with growth over the whole term, and found that less than 40 per cent of the time growth was higher in election year than before. This suggests that governments do not deliberately stimulate the economy to improve their election prospects.

Source: `Politics and Business Cycles in Industrial Democracies', Alesina, A, *Economic Policy*, 8, 1989.

Fiscal policy in practice

The multiplier process makes fiscal policy a very attractive way of boosting aggregate demand. If the economy is in recession you simply have to increase government spending and this is translated into a much larger boost to total demand. In practice, however, fiscal action is being used less and less as an instrument of macro policy, and governments are increasingly employing monetary policy instead. Why is this? For a number of reasons, the theoretical advantages of fiscal policy do not appear in practice:

1. The disparity between macro and micro aims of fiscal policy. As we saw earlier, fiscal policy is primarily a tool of microeconomic policy and using it for macro purposes can lead to conflicts.
2. Opportunities for modifying fiscal policy are limited. Many countries have only one opportunity to change their policy each year (in the Budget), while interest rates can be adjusted any time.
3. Fiscal action takes a long time to feed through the economy. Coupled with (2) above, this means that a loosening of fiscal policy intended to alleviate a current recession may serve simply to fuel a boom a few years later.
4. As shown below, tax changes today can lead to budget deficit problems tomorrow. The fear of future deficits can make fiscal policy less effective as people save more in anticipation of a reversal of current policy.

What effect do booms and recessions have on fiscal policy?

While there are problems in implementing an active fiscal policy, the tax and spending system tends to loosen or tighten automatically when the economy is entering recession or boom and so helps smooth out demand. This automatic fiscal reaction to changes in the economy occurs because many of the components of government spending and taxation are sensitive to economic conditions. When the economy is entering a recession, welfare payments rise as more people become unemployed and tax revenues fall as people's incomes decline. Forms of spending and taxation which are sensitive to the state of the economy are called *automatic stabilizers*, since they help to smooth out economic cycles automatically. Although they are convenient for stabilization purposes, they can make the business of keeping budget deficits under control more difficult by causing these to rise in recessions and fall in booms. The problems are outlined in the section on budget deficits below.

Do governments have to increase taxes to increase revenue?

Quite often, governments will spend more than they receive in tax revenue and appear impervious to pressure to reduce spending or increase taxes. They appear to believe that revenue will naturally increase and close the gap. Luckily for them this is sometimes correct, as tax revenue does indeed exhibit a tendency to grow more rapidly than the economy itself — particularly in a period of inflation. If the tax system is progressive (ie those on higher incomes pay proportionally more tax), the fact that inflation will tend to increase nominal incomes (but not real incomes) means that people will be brought into higher tax brackets. Even if the government acts regularly to uprate nominal tax brackets to allow for inflation, an economy growing in real terms will generate even quicker growth in tax revenue because real income improvement will also push people into higher tax brackets. This phenomenon is called *fiscal drag* (or *real fiscal drag* when full allowance is made for inflation). It is fiscal drag that allows governments to ignore relatively small budget deficits. Larger deficits can lead to changes in the stance of fiscal policy, with important implications for both individuals and firms.

Budget deficits

The judgement as to when a deficit is large enough to predicate fiscal policy changes is a key ingredient in economic forecasting. Unless the economy is growing very strongly, a tightening in fiscal policy will tend to depress growth for a year or so. The key in judging if a deficit has become too large is to ask how easily it can be financed.

Financing deficits

Budget deficits can be financed in three ways — by simply printing money; by issuing government debt (bonds); or by selling public assets. In equation form:

$$BU = DM + DB + AS$$

where BU = budget deficit
       DM = money creation (printing money)
       DB = sales of government debt
       AS = government asset sales (eg through privatization)

In developed economies, the printing of money makes little contribution to deficit financing largely because the use of cash is quite limited. On the other hand, asset sales such as privatization programmes have become important. Such sales consist of selling some potentially profit-making part of the government sector to the private sector. The government thereby effectively exchanges future revenues from these industries for a one-off payment. However, by far the most important method of deficit financing is the sale of government debt in the form of bonds.

How do governments borrow money?

Government deficits can be very large indeed: countries such as Italy and Belgium have outstanding borrowings far larger in value than the total annual output of their economies. How is such borrowing financed? The standard way for governments to finance their borrowing is by issuing bonds. A bond is a promise to pay a fixed stream of payments in the future in return for cash today. A conventional bond will pay both a series of coupons and a single redemption payment. For example, a bond called 5 per cent 2020 with a face value of £100 will pay a coupon of £5 per year until the year 2020, when the bond is redeemed and the holder receives £100.

How much will someone pay for such a bond? Although the bond in the example above had a face (or nominal) value of £100, that does not mean that a government can sell that bond for £100. The price of such a bond will depend on what alternative investment the purchaser could make. For example, if investors thought that three-month interest rates would average 10 per cent until 2020, they would pay less than £100 for the bond. Clearly, if they pay less for a bond the coupon payments will be worth more than 5 per cent and the redemption payment will be greater than the price they paid for the bond. This effect will mean that the bond's yield (ie the percentage return on the bond at its market price rather than its face value) will make it comparable with the expected return on other financial assets.

Can a country ever go bankrupt?

By borrowing money, a government can gain popularity by combining high spending with low taxation. Clearly this cannot go on for ever, since the stock of debt and the associated interest payments will one day become intolerable.

At what point does a budget deficit become unsustainable? A country can run a small deficit indefinitely, but this obtains only so long as the stock of debt is not growing more quickly than the economy itself. An increasing stock of debt will then be offset by a continually increasing tax revenue from the growing economy. In other words, the government has an asset (future tax revenue) that is growing in line with its increasing liability (the stock of debt). The size of deficit the government can run indefinitely is not easy to calculate, but estimates for the UK put the figure at around 2 per cent of GDP.

What would happen if the government attempted to run deficits greater than those sustainable in the long run? The extreme option would be to default on the debt. While this is most unlikely in a developed economy, it has already happened in a number of Third World countries.

Two other courses of action are available to bring an unsustainable deficit under control. The first is simply to undertake some form of fiscal tightening (increased taxation and/or reduced spending). The second is to generate inflation. This helps solve the problem in two ways:

1. Inflation increases government revenue from printing money (called *seigniorage*) because higher inflation increases the demand for notes and coins.
2. Inflation reduces the real value of the government's debt.

The second of these is by far the more important in most developed economies (where the use of cash is quite limited compared with cheques, bank transfers, etc). It works because inflation increases the nominal value of tax revenue while leaving the nominal value of the stock of debt unchanged.

To take an example, let us suppose that a government faces a stock of debt of £100 billion which, at an interest rate of 10 per cent, produces a debt service requirement of £10 billion per year. If total tax revenue is £20 billion per year, then 50 per cent of total tax revenue will be required for debt service. Now let us imagine that the government manages to engineer an increase in inflation which causes prices to double over a few years. As a result, total tax revenue will probably also double to £40 billion. Since the value of the stock of debt is still £100 billion, debt service at £10 billion now represents only 25 per cent of total tax revenue. The government has thus managed to halve the proportion of tax revenue needed to service its debt. In other words, it has eroded the debt through inflation. Higher inflation also means more fiscal drag and more government revenue from printing money. It is therefore clear that governments have a strong incentive to generate inflation when faced with a large debt burden.

Structural and cyclical deficits

Some government deficits and surpluses are due to the state of the economy itself. As we saw earlier, government revenue tends to fall and spending to rise automatically when the economy is in recession (the opposite occurs in a boom). Accordingly, the government deficit will also tend to rise during a recession and fall during a boom. Such deficit changes are only temporary and are very different from deficits created by deliberate government action. Economists refer to either *structural* or *cyclical* deficits — the latter being that part of the deficit caused by the current state of the economy.

The structural deficit can be measured in many ways, but is basically defined as the deficit that would occur if the output gap were zero, ie the economy were at potential. The cyclical deficit is then the remainder of the deficit.

Table 4.2 *Deficits and structural deficits in 1992 (percentage of GDP)*

	Total deficit	Structural deficit
United States	−4.5	−4.0
Japan	0.7	0.9
Germany	−2.6	−4.5
France	−3.9	−2.8
Italy	−9.5	−8.6
United Kingdom	−6.2	−3.5
Canada	−6.6	−3.3

Source: *OECD Economic Outlook,* December 1993

Table 4.2 shows estimates of the structural component of deficits for a number of countries. Cyclical effects can be quite a large component of any deficit, but economists are far more interested in structural deficits. The reason for this is simple. Since we know that recessions and booms tend to be only temporary (although temporary in this case can mean over ten years!) the government need not take any explicit action to deal with the cyclical deficits which they generate. It can continue to borrow during the recession and wait until the economy picks up before paying the debt back. Structural deficits, on the other hand, may grow and grow unless the government takes specific action to deal with them.

Deficits and expectations

If a government uses inflation to reduce the real value of its debt, people who previously bought government bonds lose money since the real value of the bond has gone down. So if purchasers of government bonds suspect that the government will use inflation to help get rid of a large structural deficit, they will ask for better terms in the form of a higher interest rate. In practice, there is usually a correlation between the actual size of government deficits and the interest rates governments have to pay on their debt.

This correlation is a clear example of the importance of expectations on people's behaviour. If governments can convince prospective purchasers of government bonds that they will not create inflation, they can substantially reduce the cost of their debt service through the reduced interest rates on their bonds.

A concept called *Ricardian equivalence* further illustrates the importance of expectations in the area of fiscal policy. This idea assumes that people are extremely forward-looking in their behaviour and conclude that if the government loosens fiscal policy (ie increases spending or reduces taxation), it must tighten that policy some time in the future in order to bring the budget deficit back into line. (Of course, in this sort of forward-looking world, the possibility that governments could conceivably create unexpected inflation is ruled out — people are not fooled by that trick!) Thus, anticipating future tightening, people may increase their savings today to help finance the period of future tight policy and thereby counteract the effect of the policy loosening. On these assumptions, the increase in private savings is therefore equivalent to the increase in public borrowing.

The assumptions underlying the concept of Ricardian equivalence are quite extreme. They require individuals not only to be sophisticated enough to foresee exactly the future consequences of current government actions, but also to act upon those expectations, thereby offsetting current government policy. However, if the budget deficit looks very large, it is reasonable to anticipate policy tightening. Such expectations can cause fiscal policy to be significantly less effective than the simple multiplier model outlined earlier.

Estimates of the likely effect of fiscal policy changes on the economy must take some account of people's expectations. If the government has been running a big deficit for many years, then when it does actually tighten fiscal policy the impact on the economy may be quite small because people would have anticipated the change and so prepared for it (eg by saving more). An unanticipated change in fiscal policy is likely to have a far bigger impact.

Summary

1. The main aim of public expenditure is to allow for government intervention in areas where the free market does not work efficiently, such as public goods and natural monopolies.

2. Taxation, on the other hand, seeks to raise revenue with minimal distortion to the market and without reducing the incentive to work.

3. A given increase in government spending or reduction in taxes will increase demand more than one for one because of the multiplier effect. However, various factors, including the long lags involved in implementing fiscal policy, mean that it is rarely used as an instrument of macroeconomic policy.

4. Fortunately, fiscal factors automatically help stimulate aggregate demand in recessions through automatic stabilizers.

5. The major macroeconomic constraint on fiscal policy is the budget deficit and changes in fiscal policy will often result from a desire to stabilize the deficit.

6. If a deficit is cyclical or relatively small, then a change in fiscal policy may not be required because future growth will eliminate it automatically.

7. Budget deficits can also be reduced by inflation, and a country with a large budget deficit has a strong incentive to create inflation.

8. Because most people realise that a large budget deficit is an indicator of future fiscal tightening, the tightening when it occurs may have less effect than at other times.

Questions for consideration

1. In country A people save 10 per cent of their income, the tax rate is 20 per cent and the propensity to import is 2 per cent. In country B the propensity to save is 10 per cent, the tax rate is 20 per cent, but the propensity to import is 14 per cent. In which country does fiscal policy have a greater effect on the economy? How big is the multiplier effect in each country?
2. If a country has a budget deficit of 1 per cent of GDP, should it tighten fiscal policy to get rid of the deficit altogether? If it runs a deficit of that size at the peak of an economic boom, does that change your answer?
3. Why might you expect the ability of an increase in income taxes to reduce the budget deficit to be less when income taxes are already very high?
4. Why might you expect a country with a large budget deficit to have high inflation? Would your answer be different if the government's existing debt were index linked (ie if it had issued bonds that pay more when inflation is higher)?
5. What effect does privatization have on the government deficit? Why might privatization increase future budget deficits?

Further reading

A detailed account of UK fiscal policy is given each year in *The Financial Statement and Budget Report* (FSBR), published by HMSO. This is the published form of the Budget given in November. An assessment of likely Budget measures and the economic situation in general is given in *The Green Budget*, published by the Institute of Fiscal Studies just before the FSBR.

On taxation see *The UK Tax System* by J Kay and M King (Oxford University Press, 1986). An analysis of budget deficits is given in 'A guide to public sector debt and deficits' by W Buiter (*Economic Policy*, 1, 1985). A collection of studies of public debt problems appear in *High Public Debt: The Italian Experience* by F Giavazzi and L Spaventa (Cambridge University Press, 1988).

5

Monetary policy

The aims of this chapter are to explain:

1. the role of interest rates and money supply in monetary policy;
2. how to predict future monetary policy;
3. the role of credibility in monetary policy;
4. how monetary and fiscal policy interact.

Monetary policy, or the government's decisions about interest rates and money supply, is the most actively used means of influencing output and inflation. This is because changes in monetary policy are both easy to implement and very effective in economies with a highly developed financial system.

Although in this chapter we shall refer to the monetary policy-making authority as the Central Bank, in many countries the Central Bank simply implements monetary policy decisions made by the government (see box on page 82).

What is monetary policy?

There is often a confusion about what monetary policy actually is. Some people take monetary policy to mean the Central Bank's decisions about interest rates, others take it to mean money supply targets and the money supply in general. In fact both are right, since the supply of money and interest rates (ie the price of money) are directly linked.

In practice, it is by controlling the supply of certain types of money (called *high-powered* or *base money*) that the Central Bank gains control of the price of money, ie short-term interest rates (also called *money-market interest rates*). Figure 5.1 shows how, by controlling the supply of money, the Central Bank can manipulate the level of interest rates for a given demand for money. Changes in the supply of money are often called *open market operations* since they transfer money between the Central Bank and the open market. By slightly reducing the quantity of base money (through open market operations) the Central Bank can increase interest rates from, say, 6 to 7 per cent.

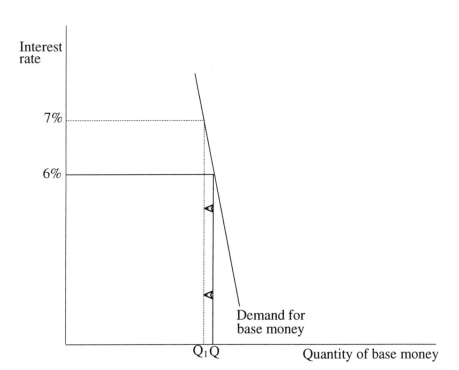

Figure 5.1   *How Central Banks set interest rates*

As we shall see, the Central Bank actually only controls that small part of the total money supply called base money. However, this part (which includes notes and coins) is very important, since all other forms of money must be convertible back into base money.

The Central Bank can set any price it likes for supplying this type of money, because the commercial banks and the economy in general cannot function without it. In the conduct of open market operations the Central Bank sets the price (the short-term interest rate) and must then supply as much as the economy demands at that price. In some countries (Switzerland, for example) Central Banks choose to supply a fixed amount of base money to the economy and allow interest rates to be determined in the market by demand. This method of setting monetary policy is called *monetary base control*.

Money supply

For many years, economists were caricatured as coming from one of two warring factions. They were either Keynesians or monetarists. The essential difference between them was that the monetarists believed the purpose of macroeconomic policy was to keep the money supply under control. The Keynesians, on the other hand, were supposed to be more interested in stabilizing growth directly and ignored the money supply. In fact, there is little dispute among economists over the role of the money supply. They accept that inflation is clearly related to the money supply (more money and the same number of goods mean higher prices). They also agree that targeting the money supply can make economic policy more credible (see below). The problems with money supply targets are practical, ie how do you measure money and how reliable is the link between money, output and inflation?

Measuring money

One of the major difficulties encountered in implementing monetary policy and assessing monetary conditions is that there is no clear definition of exactly what constitutes the money supply. Most countries employ a number of measures of money supply, usually but not always, prefixed with the letter M (like M4 in the UK and M2 in the USA). These measures, ranging from M0 to M4, encompass increasingly broad measures of money.

There are two basic types of money that are especially important: base money and transactions money. The first is relatively easy to measure, while the second is extremely difficult.

As we have seen, *base money* (also called high-powered money, fiat money, the monetary base or M0) comprises those forms of money that are supplied solely by the Central Bank. The best known form of base money is notes and coins, the production of which is strictly controlled by the Central Bank. The other component of base money is reserve assets. These are assets which the commercial banks are required to hold by law as a fixed proportion of their total liabilities. Like notes and coins, they are strictly controlled by the Central Bank.

Base money is important for two reasons. First, it is through its sole control of this form of money that the Central Bank can control interest rates, as we described earlier. Second, since the Central Bank rarely pays interest on the constituents of the monetary base (and no Central Bank pays interest on notes and coins), an issuance of base money is like an interest-free loan to the Central Bank. Since the proceeds of this interest-free loan (called *seigniorage*) are usually paid to the government, they can be used to finance budget deficits (see Chapter 4). Increasing the supply of base money to finance government spending basically amounts to finance by printing money. This type of finance can dramatically reduce interest rates and is highly inflationary; it is the root cause of all hyperinflation.

The second and more problematic measure of money is *transactions money*. This measure is important since, if properly quantified, it can give policy-makers an early indication of inflation and growth. Most countries use some measure of money to help guide policy. This is because the growth in the total amount of money used in transactions is closely linked both to the growth in the total volume of transactions (ie real growth) and to the growth in prices (ie inflation). Increases in money holdings for transactions purposes can therefore be an early indication of increased spending and/or inflation. If this measure of money performs properly, governments can use it to guide policy. Most countries have some stated target for money supply growth, although the emphasis put on these money supply targets varies from country to country.

Transactions money is a broader measure of money than base money because it should include all forms of money that can be used to buy goods and services. Transactions money may therefore include items such as bank deposit accounts, since cheques drawn on these accounts can be used to buy goods. Unfortunately, the boundary between what does and does not constitute transactions money is extremely blurred. For example, someone with money in an interest-bearing deposit account may be holding that money as savings and not as a means of engaging in transactions. Differentiating between money held for saving and money held for use in transactions is one of the major problems in measuring transactions money.

The importance of transactions money

Even if it could be measured properly, why should policy-makers and economic observers be interested in monitoring transactions money? The answer to this question lies in the quantity equation (discussed in Chapter 3), which simply states that the value of transactions in a given time period must be exactly equal to the amount of money in circulation multiplied by the number of times that money is used for transactions in the period (ie the *velocity of circulation*). If we think of the number of transactions as the volume of output in the economy and the price of transactions as the price level in the economy, then the importance of the quantity equation becomes clear. In particular, if we accept the idea described in Chapter 3 that, in the long run, the volume of output is set by exogenous factors (such as technological progress), then the excessive growth of transactions money is a necessary condition for rising prices (inflation).

It is the link between transactions money and inflation which leads to the use of money supply targets. Pure monetarism argues that if it is the supply of transactions money which causes inflation, monetary policy is simply a matter of targeting a rate of money supply growth consistent with zero inflation. In practice things are not so simple, and although most countries attach some weight to money supply growth, few would base policy decisions on the movement of transactions money alone. There are three reasons for this:

1. The velocity of circulation is not stable. In the quantity equation, the relationship between a given amount of money and the value of transactions is directly determined by the velocity of circulation of that money. If that velocity is variable through time, then it becomes very difficult to relate a given rate of money growth to inflation. For example, interest rates have an important bearing on the velocity of circulation. High interest rates mean that holding certain types of non-interest bearing money (cash, for example) is costly. People will therefore attempt to economize on money holdings and may succeed in managing their cash-flow more efficiently.

2. Transactions money is not easily controllable. Since it includes many types of money that are not under the direct control of the Central Bank (private bank accounts, for example), it can be very difficult to hit a given money supply target. Most countries which set targets for the money supply regularly fail to achieve them.

3. There may be no useful information for policy-makers in transactions money. Although the quantity equation links money and nominal demand, it does not say which causes which. If high inflation causes people to demand more money (and not vice versa), then there is no useful information in money that is not already available in other indicators. Most countries find that there is some information value in transactions money, but that it is only one of many variables which help to predict inflation and output.

Money targeting in the UK and Germany

Should governments use money growth targets? Most major economies have some target for money supply growth. In most cases, however, the growth of money is only one of many indicators used to assess economic conditions, and governments will often ignore the message from money supply growth if other economic indicators (eg wage growth) are not telling the same story. Some economists argue that this tendency to ignore money supply growth is dangerous, as the money supply is by far the most important indicator. The experience of UK and Germany, which have at times followed money supply targets very closely, gives conflicting evidence on the benefit of targeting.

At the beginning of the 1980s the UK instituted the Medium Term Financial Strategy (MTFS). The centrepiece of this strategy was that money supply targets (for M3, a broad measure of transactions money) would be used to guide monetary policy. Target ranges were constructed on the basis of the past relationship between money growth, output and inflation (ie the velocity of circulation) so that if the targets were hit, growth and inflation would remain at desired levels. These targets were followed even when other indicators suggested that the economy was entering a deep recession. As it turned out, the other indicators were right; M3 kept growing rapidly despite the fact that output and inflation were falling. What went wrong? As Figure 5.2 shows, the UK was unlucky enough to start targeting the money supply just as the relationship between money and nominal output was changing (probably due to deregulation in the financial sector).

Germany, on the other hand, has been targeting M3 for many years and as a result has achieved both stable output growth and low and stable inflation throughout the 1980s. In Germany at least, money supply targets seem to have worked and money supply growth seems to have given some advance warning of future problems. However, as Figure 5.2 shows, German reunification (which occurred in 1990) may have disturbed the velocity of circulation and made money a less reliable indicator even in Germany.

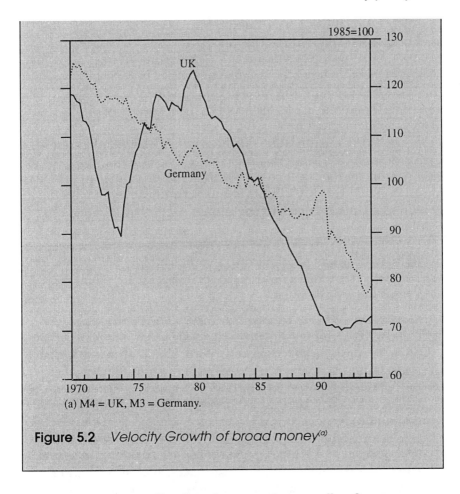

(a) M4 = UK, M3 = Germany.

Figure 5.2 *Velocity Growth of broad money*[a]

How effective is monetary policy?

When the Central Bank changes interest rates, how does this affect aggregate demand and inflation? Changes in interest rates affect activity and inflation in three ways. First, by altering the cost of borrowing, they affect the incentive to save. If the cost of credit is reduced, there is a greater incentive to borrow and bring forward expenditure, rather than save and consume in the future. In the corporate sector, lower interest rates reduce the rate of return at which capital projects become financially viable, making it more profitable to borrow and invest (these effects were discussed in Chapter 2).

Second, a cut in interest rates can influence expenditure by altering the level and distribution of income. A fall in interest rates redistributes income from savers to borrowers, which may lead to an increase in expenditure. This occurs because borrowers tend to have a higher propensity to spend. Changes in interest rates may also redistribute income by changing asset prices and wealth. Interest rates can alter the value of both financial assets (eg equities and bonds) and real assets (eg property). Changes in wealth are also likely to affect expenditure.

The third transmission mechanism operates through the exchange rate. If UK interest rates are reduced then, other things being equal, sterling will fall (see Chapter 6 for a detailed explanation). This will make UK exports more competitive and stimulate growth, but will also make imports more expensive, thus generating inflation.

In combination these three channels make monetary policy a powerful instrument for achieving macroeconomic policy aims and explains why it is more actively used than fiscal policy. It does, however, have some limitations:

1. *Short-term and long-term interest rates.* The Central Bank's control over base money only gives it control over one interest rate. Most Central Banks choose to control the shortest possible interest rate, ie the overnight rate (the rate of interest charged for borrowing money for one day). But in practice, most individuals and companies need to borrow money for longer than one day, and their decisions are therefore affected by a longer-term rate such as the three-month interest rate. This means that the effectiveness of monetary policy depends crucially on the extent to which very short-term interest rates (which the Central Bank controls) affect longer-term rates at which most people borrow and lend. The effect of short-term interest rates on longer-term interest rates is described below under the term structure of interest rates.

2. *Expectations.* As with fiscal policy, monetary policy has far less effect on the economy if it is anticipated. In particular, financial markets will often discount an expected change in interest rate so that the effect of the change when it occurs is reduced.

3. *Effects on real interest rates and output in the long run.* In the long run, monetary policy can influence neither output growth nor real interest rates. Given that monetary policy controls the interest rate and can have long-term effects on the rate of inflation, it may seem odd that the real interest rate cannot be controlled in the long run. The general principle is that demand-side policies (including monetary policy) can only work on the real economy in

the short run; it is the supply side which matters in the longer run. If the government attempts to keep real interest rates, say, 1 per cent below the long-run rate, or output, say, 1 per cent above its long-run growth rate, then inflation will tend to rise faster and faster, leading to hyperinflation. This means that in order to keep the economy on track (ie no hyperinflation or hyperdeflation), interest rates must eventually settle down to the long-run real rate of interest for the economy.

4. *Uncertain effects*. Another practical problem with monetary policy is illustrated in Table 5.1. Comparing this table with Table 4.1 on page 58 indicates that, although all the models show a 1 per cent interest rate change having a greater impact on GDP than a 1 per cent tax change, the estimated effects vary hugely between the models. This is not simply a problem for macro models. Generally speaking, economists know less about how monetary policy affects the economy than fiscal policy. Predicting the effects of a given change in monetary policy is consequently very difficult.

Table 5.1 *The effect of a 1 per cent increase in interest rates on output and inflation*

| | Percentage change in GDP and inflation according to: | | | | | |
| | Treasury model | | London Business School model | | NIESR model | |
	GDP	Inf.	GDP	Inf.	GDP	Inf.
Year 1	–0.4%	0.4%	–0.3%	0.0%	–0.4%	–0.4%
Year 2	–0.9%	–0.1%	–0.8%	–0.5%	–0.6%	–1.1%
Year 3	–1.3%	–0.6%	–0.8%	–0.8%	–0.4%	–0.1%
Year 4	–1.5%	–1.2%	–0.3%	–0.8%	–0.1%	0.7%
Year 5	–1.5%	–1.7%	0.3%	–0.1%	0.0%	0.8%

Source: *Warwick University Ready Reckoner*, 1993

The term structure of interest rates

What is the best way of predicting future interest rates? Since the relationship between long-term and short-term interest rates is determined primarily by market expectations, predictions are relatively easy to derive. For example, consider an investor who wants to invest money for two years. He or she can either settle for the two-year interest rate, or invest the money for one year and then reinvest a year later at the one-year interest prevailing in a year's time. Since financial markets operate so as to make the informed investor indifferent between these two options (markets do not readily offer easy opportunities to make excess profits), we can derive a forecast of one-year interest rates in one year's time by comparing one- and two-year interest rates today (see Figure 5.3).

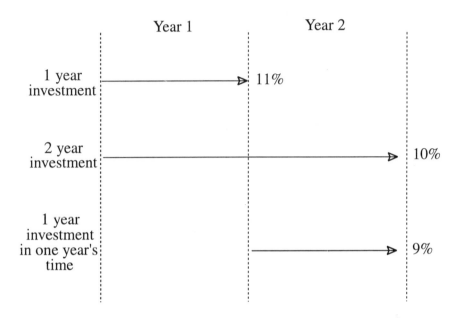

Figure 5.3   *Deriving expectations of future interest rates*

If investors think they can get the same rate of return by investing for one year at 11 per cent and two years at 10 per cent, they must expect that the one-year interest rate in one year's time will be 9 per cent.

The relationship between long-term and short-term interest rates, also called the *term structure of interest rates*, offers economists a useful means of deriving market expectations of future interest rates. It also gives a guide to expected future inflation because, as we noted above, expected real interest rates are relatively stable in the medium to long term (ie about 5 years and beyond). For example, if long-term interest rates are above short-term rates, financial markets are probably expecting interest rates and inflation to rise.

The yield curve

Because financial markets aim to seek out all profit-making opportunities, it is unlikely that the return on investing in a two-year asset will differ very much from the return on a one-year asset plus the expected return on a one-year asset in one year's time. This means that we can judge market expectations of future short-term (eg one-year) interest rates by looking at the market price of long-term assets. The best assets to use for this purpose are government bonds. This is because (a) governments are unlikely to go bankrupt so there is no problem with credit risk; and (b) the government debt market is usually the biggest and most liquid market in long-term assets.

As Figure 5.4 shows, by looking at the yields (ie the rate of return on bonds) on individual government bonds and fitting a curve through all the points, it is possible to come up with a good estimate of market expectations of future interest rates. This estimate is called the *yield curve*. The yield curve gives an estimate of average expected interest rates (eg the 20-year yield is the average short-term expected interest rate over the next 20 years). It is possible to transform this average rate into *implied forward rates* which give the expected one-year interest rate at various times (eg the one-year interest rate expected in 20 years' time).

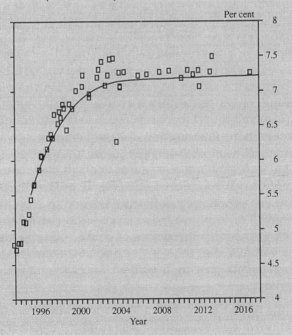

Figure 5.4 *Bank of England's yield curve*

> Figure 5.4 shows the Bank of England's yield curve that has been fitted to the observed yields on UK government bonds. As well as fitting a smooth line through the yields, the yield curve estimation adjusts for factors such as tax.
>
> Of course, there are a number of factors, such as risk (long-term assets tend to have more volatile prices), that mean that the yield curve is not a totally reliable measure of market expectations. However, it gives a good approximation and is closely monitored by forecasters and policy-makers.

Monetary policy and credibility

The importance of expectations in monetary policy, illustrated in the previous section, means that credibility (or making people believe what you say) is of central importance to policy-makers. This is for three main reasons:

1. *Credibility makes monetary policy more effective.* If markets believe that the current interest rate will be maintained, then longer-term interest rates will move in line with short-term interest rates and monetary policy will affect all borrowers and lenders, not just those who use short-term interest rates.
2. *Credibility helps to control deficits.* As we saw in the previous chapter, if the government deficit is large, the government may have an incentive to print more money as a way of funding spending. This has the effect of cutting short-term interest rates but increasing longer-term rates (because people expect inflation to increase which must, sooner or later, mean higher interest rates). If a government is doing most of its borrowing at longer-term interest rates (as most governments do), then the greater its credibility the lower the interest rate at which it has to borrow.
3. *Credibility helps to control inflation.* If people believe that the government's monetary policy is designed to keep inflation low, workers will tend not to make large wage claims and firms will not seek to push up the prices of goods they produce (because neither will fear that other price and cost increases will reduce their real earnings or their profits). Such a reaction is itself anti-inflationary.

In spite of the enormous importance of credibility to policy-makers, it is extremely difficult to achieve. Governments try hard to persuade people that they are committed to reducing inflation, but people know that governments also have a very strong incentive to renege on any commitments they make. That incentive stems mainly from the fact that, in the short run, running a loose monetary policy can be beneficial because it tends to act on output and employment before it affects inflation. Accordingly, there can be a short period when a loose monetary policy can increase output and reduce unemployment without inflation being affected, thereby briefly achieving any government's ideal outcome — non-inflationary growth. This short-period gain is attractive to governments, particularly on the eve of an election. Of course, the benefit is only short-lived and quite soon inflation will start to rise and output and employment growth will fall back to the rate of growth of productive potential. Because of the very existence of this incentive, residual scepticism is always likely even of a government apparently committed to a credible anti-inflationary monetary policy.

Achieving credibility

Since credibility is invaluable but so difficult to acquire, governments have attempted to implement monetary policy in a manner calculated to help to increase credibility. They have proved willing to give up the luxury of being able to determine policy for short-term reasons simply to enhance the credibility of overall policy. Two main methods have been used:

1. *Binding policy rules.* If the government can bind itself to a simple and verifiable policy rule, then people will more willingly believe that policy will not be set for short-term reasons. Two types of policy mechanisms have been employed: money supply targets and exchange rate targets. Money supply targets have been used in a number of countries. They require the government to keep money supply growth within a given target range. The problem is that money supply may not be a good indicator of economic conditions and so inappropriate policy may therefore result. Exchange rate targets have an advantage over money supply targets in that they allow a government to tie its performance to another economy with a proven record of low inflation (see Chapters 6 and 8). However, controlling the relevant exchange rate is not always easy and many countries, including the UK, are now adopting inflation targets.
2. *Central Bank independence.* By making the Central Bank independent, governments effectively give up short-run control of monetary policy. Through setting the terms of independence, the elected government can ensure that the independent Central Bank sets monetary policy in an appropriate way. However, this

may cause people to doubt that the Central Bank is free from government interference and that monetary policy is truly independent of political influence. On the other hand, a fully independent Central Bank may be so independent that its policies do not appear to be in the public interest. For example, an independent Central Bank may be so keen on keeping inflation down that it may keep policy tighter than necessary and thus suppress growth.

Do independent Central Banks deliver lower inflation?

Over the last few years a number of Central Banks (such as the Banque de France) have been made independent of their governments. The main reason for doing this is that an independent Central Bank is supposed to deliver greater credibility and lower inflation. Have independent Central Banks delivered?

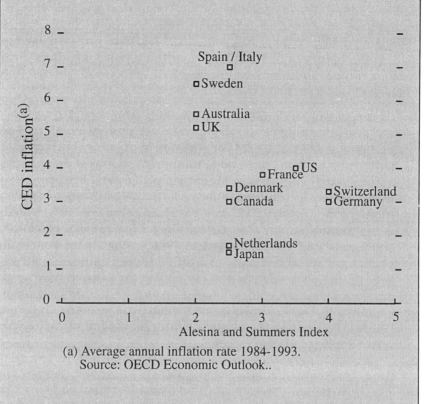

(a) Average annual inflation rate 1984-1993.
Source: OECD Economic Outlook..

Figure 5.5 *Central Bank independence and inflation*

Alesina and Summers looked at this question by constructing an index of independence (based on factors such as the role of the government in appointing Central Bank governors) and comparing it with average inflation across countries. Their results, illustrated in Figure 5.5, seem to indicate that the more independent Central Banks have indeed delivered lower inflation. However, interpreting their results is complicated by the fact that countries (like, for example, Germany) whose electorate tends to be more averse to inflation than other countries will also tend to give their Central Banks independence as a sort of insurance. The key question is, would those countries have had lower inflation anyway? This leaves the case for independence unproven.

Source: 'Central Bank Independence and Macroeconomic Performance: Some Comparative Evidence', Alesina, A and Summers, L, *Journal of Money, Credit and Banking*, May, 1993.

Fiscal policy and monetary policy

In the last two chapters we have treated fiscal policy and monetary policy as independent. In practice they cannot be formulated independently of each other, for two basic reasons:

1. *Balancing policy.* Fiscal and monetary policy have similar effects on the economy: a loosening of either stimulates demand and so raises growth and inflation. This means that if overall policy is aimed at achieving certain economic targets, then both instruments must be balanced in such a way as to achieve those targets. This is equally true of money supply and the exchange rate as well as growth or inflation targets. One simple way to think about this is through the concept of *crowding out*. Crowding out can occur when the government borrows to finance a fiscal expansion. Such borrowing crowds out private sector borrowing and results in excess demand for funds, which puts upward pressure on interest rates. The fact that fiscal and monetary policy can, in practice, be balanced against each other (eg looser fiscal policy offset by tighter monetary policy) does not mean that policy-makers should be indifferent as to which instrument they use to achieve their targets. Each can have very different effects (see box on Reaganomics on page 98). The interaction between monetary and fiscal policy is also demonstrated in IS-LM analysis (see box below).

2.   *Financing deficits.* As we saw in Chapter 4, printing money is one
     way of financing budget deficits. Its use entails an increase in the
     supply of base money and a reduction in interest rates. Although
     this form of financing is less important in developed economies
     where the demand for cash is quite limited, loosening monetary
     policy can also help finance deficits by reducing the real value of
     debt.

IS-LM analysis

In many economics textbooks the interaction of monetary
and fiscal policy is described by using IS-LM analysis. An IS-LM
diagram is shown in Figure 5.6. The idea is that the IS curve is
supposed to show combinations of interest rates and output
that are consistent with a balance between investment and
savings. The LM curve shows combinations of interest rates
and output where money supply is in balance with the
demand for money. The whole economy is in balance where
these two curves cross. These curves can then be used to
show what happens when either monetary or fiscal policy is
changed. For example, an increase in government spending
increases output through the multiplier effect, but it also
increases interest rates, for a given supply of money, because
of 'crowding out'. This is shown by shifting the IS curve to the
right. Increasing the supply of base money is shown by shifting
the LM curve to the right, which decreases interest rates and
increases output.

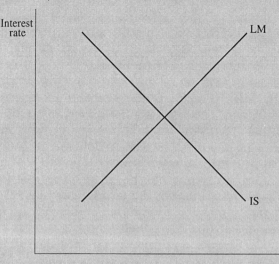

Figure 5.6   *IS-LM diagram*

IS-LM analysis has a number of drawbacks. It says nothing about the effects of policy on inflation or the exchange rate. It assumes that monetary policy is operated through a fixed money supply rule (that is why interest rates rise when fiscal policy is loosened). Few countries operate a fixed money supply rule in practice. For these reasons, and the fact that it seems an overly complicated way of expressing some simple ideas, we have not used IS-LM analysis in this book, although you will find it in almost all other macroeconomic textbooks.

Summary

1. Central Banks control interest rates through adjusting the supply of base money. Base money (M0) is different from transactions money, such as M3 or M4, which some Central Banks also choose to target.

2. The value of money supply targets depends on the stability of the velocity of circulation of money.

3. Although monetary policy is easier to implement than fiscal policy, its effects can be unpredictable.

4. The easiest way of predicting future changes in interest rates is to look at the slope of the yield curve. Since real interest rates are fixed in the long run, the yield curve also gives some indications about future inflation.

5. If a Central Bank has credibility, using monetary policy to keep inflation down becomes much easier. Mechanisms that help create credibility include simple policy rules (such as money supply targets) and Central Bank independence.

6. Fiscal and monetary policy interact because they can both be used to achieve the same aims (low inflation and stable growth). Loose monetary policy (printing money) can also be used to finance budget deficits.

Questions for consideration

1. If interest rates are 12 per cent and inflation is expected to be 5 per cent, what is the level of real interest rates?
2. If the Central Bank deliberately increased the supply of base money through open market operations, what effect would this have on interest rates? And what effect would it have on inflation and growth?
3. What effect would a Central Bank announcement that it wished to reduce inflation have on long-term interest rates if (a) the Central Bank had high credibility (ie financial markets believed what the Central Bank said); or (b) the Central Bank had low credibility?
4. If a Central Bank had a fixed money supply target and the velocity of circulation fell unexpectedly, what would happen to inflation and growth?
5. If the yield curve was upward sloping, what could you infer about expected future interest rates? Could you infer anything about expected future inflation?

Further reading

An assessment of UK monetary policy is given once a quarter in the Bank of England's *Inflation Report*. This also gives market interest rate and inflation expectations based on yield curves.

A good overview of monetary policy and the monetary system is given in *Money, Information and Uncertainty* (C Goodhart, MIT Press, 1989).

6

The exchange rate

The aims of this chapter are to explain:

1. current theories of how the exchange rate is determined;
2. how the exchange rate affects the economy;
3. the role of the exchange rate in macroeconomic policy.

When international trade makes up a significant proportion of a country's economic activity, the exchange rate is one of the most important determinants of both inflation and output. It also has a major impact on firms competing in overseas markets, and even on firms with foreign competitors in the home market. Not surprisingly, the exchange rate is therefore the most closely monitored economic variable. Unfortunately, it is also the most volatile and unpredictable.

Before looking in detail at the determination of the exchange rate, a few definitions are required:

Bilateral exchange rate

A bilateral exchange rate is simply the exchange rate between the currencies of two countries, such as the US dollar/sterling or the French franc/Deutschmark exchange rate. Given its two-sided nature, one needs to be clear about what is meant by a fall or rise in this exchange rate. A fall in the exchange rate is always taken to mean a fall in the value of the local in terms of the foreign currency, but this can lead to statements such as, 'the franc fell from 10 to 11 against the pound'. This apparent contradiction arises because any quoted bilateral rate is calculated by dividing the smaller currency unit into the larger unit, so that the quoted rate is always greater than one. As a result, international comparative rates for most major currencies are quoted in terms of the US dollar (a relatively large currency unit), except for sterling (a larger unit) which is quoted in dollars per pound.

Trade weighted or effective exchange rate

The effective exchange rate index for a country is a weighted average of its bilateral exchange rates. The weights are calculated in relation to the importance of each country's foreign trade. The trade-weighted exchange rate is of great importance in macroeconomic terms, since it captures the effect of all the bilateral rates on the economy. The weights are calculated by the International Monetary Fund (IMF) using estimates of trade that include the impact of indirect competition in third markets and thus reflect the importance of each country in the trade of all other countries.

Real exchange rate

The real exchange rate is simply the exchange rate adjusted for relative inflation. The formula used is:

$$EXR = EX^*P/PO \text{ or } DEXR = DEX^*INF/INFO$$

where EXR =   real exchange rate (DEXR = change in the real
           exchange rate)
  EX   =   exchange rate (DEX = change in the exchange rate)
  PO   =   overseas price level (INFO = inflation overseas)
  P   =   local price level (INF = local inflation)

The importance of the real exchange rate is that it reflects the competitiveness of home-produced goods. It compares the price of a good in one country directly with its price in another, and allows for the fact that high inflation or a rise in a country's nominal exchange rate both make its goods more expensive overseas.

What determines the exchange rate in the short run?

Table 6.1   *Gross daily turnover in the foreign exchange market (1992 average daily turnover by currency, billions of dollars)*

US dollar	1114
Deutschmark	544
Yen	313
Pound sterling	185
Swiss franc	116

Source: BIS Survey

The foreign exchange market is by far the largest financial market in the world, as table 6.1 shows. Daily turnover averages $2.7 trillion a day. Clearly, this level of turnover is far larger than is needed simply to finance international trade and tourism. This is because the foreign exchange market — and as a result the exchange rate — is dominated by financial flows seeking the highest rate of return. The exchange rate is therefore almost impossible to predict on a day-to-day basis. There are, however, some general principles that can be used to help predict trends in exchange rates.

The most widely accepted theory about the short-run determination of the exchange rate is based on the principle that the exchange rate moves so as to equalize the rate of return on assets in different countries. For example, if interest rates were (and were expected to remain at) 10 per cent in the UK and 5 per cent in the US, then a fall in sterling of 5 per cent against the dollar over the year would even out the difference in interest rates in local currency terms. This can be expressed in equation form as:

$$DE = Rf - Rl$$

where Rl = rate of return on local (own currency) asset
Rf = rate of return on foreign asset
DE = change in the exchange rate between the two countries

This follows directly from the way in which financial markets price forward contracts in foreign exchange. In the *forward market* (ie the market for the delivery of foreign exchange at a prearranged rate on a prearranged date), the future exchange rate used is determined by the formula shown above. To see why, imagine that you need a bank to deliver DM 1 million in one year's time. The safest thing for the bank to do is to buy the DM today, invest them for a year and then deliver them to you. If the interest rate in Germany were the same as that in the UK, it could do this at no cost (since the return would be the same as if it had kept the money in sterling). In this case, the bank could deliver the DM to you at the end of the year at today's exchange rate (plus its commission, of course). However, if interest rates were lower in Germany than in the UK, say 5 per cent in Germany and 10 per cent in the UK, the bank would lose money over the year. It would cover this loss by contracting to deliver the DM to you at a rate 5 per cent worse than today's rate.

The theory of exchange rate determination that is based on this principle is called *uncovered interest parity* (UIP). This theory simply states that the forward exchange rate derived from the forward market is the best predictor of future exchange rates.

How well does the UIP theory of exchange rate determination work in practice?

There are two major difficulties associated with the UIP theory of exchange rate movements.

At first sight, a theory of exchange rate determination that seeks to relate exchange rate movements to interest rate differentials, which are relatively stable, cannot also explain the much higher volatility of exchange rates.

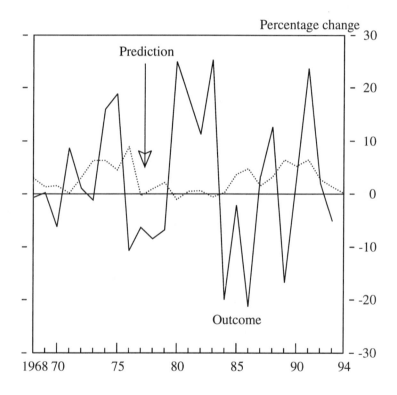

Figure 6.1 *UIP predictions and the exchange rate (Sterling/Dollar)*

Certainly, on the basis of Figure 6.1, it does not appear that UIP does a good job of predicting exchange rate movements. However, proponents of the UIP theory argue that the high volatility in observed exchange rates is due to the phenomenon of *overshooting*. This occurs whenever participants in the foreign exchange market change their view about future interest rates without changing their opinion as to the long-run level at which the exchange rate should settle. Since UIP links the future change in the exchange rate to relative interest rates, if the interest rate in one country is expected to go up then the exchange rate will jump to a point from which it can depreciate to its long-run level (what determines its long run level is described below). This effect is illustrated in Figure 6.2.

This example of exchange rate overshooting shows how a change in market expectation of future interest rates can cause the exchange rate to jump by 10 per cent. The jump allows the exchange rate to fall in the future to reflect actual interest differentials.

Thus, since overshooting and hence exchange rate volatility occur as a result of anticipated interest rate movements, it can be held that volatility is consistent with the UIP theory.

A more serious problem for the UIP theory is that, in some countries, the rate of change of the exchange rate differs from that predicted by interest rate differentials — even over long periods. Although over a short period divergences from UIP can be

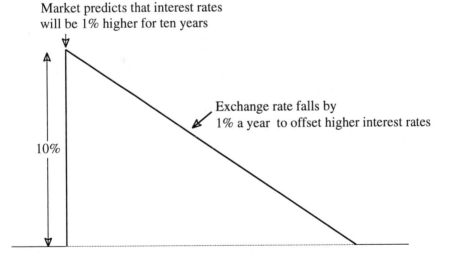

Figure 6.2   *Overshooting*

explained by overshooting, it is hard to believe that financial markets can be consistently wrong for long periods. The reason given for this long-term divergence from UIP is that some currencies are seen to be more risky than others. Since most financial agents are averse to taking excessive risk, a currency that is perceived as being more risky (ie more volatile) must pay more to entice investors; in other words, they must pay a *risk premium*. For example, UK assets pay more than German assets through higher interest rates to attract foreign investors, because sterling is perceived as being a less stable currency.

Despite these problems, comparing interest rate differentials offers a relatively sound method of predicting the general trend in the exchange rate. For instance, it suggests that although unexpected changes in interest rates will cause the exchange rates to jump unpredictably, if a country's interest rates are generally higher than others, its exchange rate will tend to weaken over time.

What determines the exchange rate in the long run?

The previous section showed how UIP can be used to help predict the likely change in exchange rates over time, but what predicts the long-run level at which it will settle? The most commonly used theory of the long-run path of the exchange rate is called the *purchasing power parity* (PPP) theory. This theory is based on the notion that the price of identical goods should be the same in different countries. For example, if wheat costs $10 a kilo in the US and £5 a kilo in the UK, then the PPP exchange rate that makes the price of wheat the same in both countries would be $2 to £1. If inflation is higher in one country, then the PPP exchange rate will tend to change over time and will relate to one real exchange rate (ie the exchange rate adjusted for relative inflation).

How realistic is PPP?

The idea behind PPP is that if prices between countries are misaligned, then resulting trade between the countries will tend to equalize prices. For example, if the sterling price of US wheat were much lower than UK wheat, buyers in the UK would choose imported US wheat, thereby pushing up the price of US wheat and reducing the price of UK wheat until the two prices were equal.

However, in practice, there are three main reasons why this simplified PPP relationship may not hold:

1. *Costs of transport and different import taxation regimes.* The impact of these in terms of higher costs may mean that an observed price differential for the same product in different countries cannot be profitably exploited by trade.
2. *Differences in quality and type of product.* Goods produced in two different countries may not be comparable (even wheat produced in two different countries may be of a different quality and type). Moreover, a substantial number of goods are exclusively produced in one country. Establishing PPP exchange rates is therefore extremely difficult.
3. *Non-traded goods.* A large number of goods, particularly those produced by service industries, cannot be traded. For example, it is difficult to imagine an international market for haircuts (in fact, this is simply an extreme example of the effect of transport costs).

As a result, PPP is unlikely to work even in the medium term. However, most economists would accept that it is still the most plausible explanation of what fundamentally determines exchange rates in the long run, and can therefore be used to help predict where they will settle.

Measuring PPP exchange rates

PPP exchange rates are usually measured be comparing the prices of an identical basket of goods in different countries and finding the exchange rate at which the basket costs the same. International organizations such as the Organization for Economic Cooperation and Development (OECD) and the IMF publish such measures. It is also possible to construct PPP rates by comparing the prices of just one standard good; *The Economist* magazine regularly publishes such rates based on comparing the price of McDonald's 'Big Mac' across countries!

A very different approach to measuring PPP is based on the idea that a country whose exchange rate is above PPP will tend to have a balance of payments deficit (because its goods are too expensive relative to other countries). If an overvalued exchange rate is the sole cause of deficits, then the PPP exchange rate will be the rate at which the balance of payments is in balance. So by looking at a country's balance of payments and calculating what change in competitiveness would bring it into balance, it is possible to obtain an estimate of PPP. This method of calculating PPP is also called the *fundamental equilibrium exchange rate* (FEER).

Although they are easier to calculate than standard PPP measures, FEERs present a number of problems, not least the fact the countries may run balance of payments deficits (or surpluses) for reasons other than an overvalued (or undervalued) exchange rate.

Predicting exchange rates

By looking at relative interest rates and rough estimates of PPP it is possible to obtain a general idea of exchange rate trends. Unfortunately, such trends are likely to be overshadowed by essentially unpredictable short-run volatility. Accordingly, the best bet for a firm exposed to significant foreign exchange risk is not to try to guess future exchange rate movements, but to use a forward contract.

The macroeconomic impact of the exchange rate

The exchange rate has a major influence on open economies (like most European countries), and since most of the effect of an independent change in the exchange rate occurs with a lag, monitoring the exchange rate — particularly the trade-weighted exchange rate — can give important information about future growth, inflation and the balance of payments.

Inflation and the exchange rate

The link between the exchange rate and inflation centres on the price of imported goods. If the exchange rate falls, the price of imported goods is likely to go up. This is because following a fall in the exchange rate — a fall in sterling, for example — foreign firms must either put up the sterling price of the goods they sell into the UK market or see their local currency revenue fall. In practice, they will tend to keep their local currency prices relatively constant and allow the sterling price to rise.

The consequent increase in the sterling price of imports puts upward pressure on inflation in two ways: directly, by putting up the price of imported consumer goods (which may allow UK producers to do the same); and indirectly, by putting up the price of imported raw materials (oil, for example) causing UK producers also to put up their prices. In fact, if PPP is to hold in the long run, any fall in the exchange rate must eventually lead to an exactly offsetting rise in prices. In other words, the real exchange rate (the exchange rate adjusted for relative inflation) must, in the long run, be unaffected by changes in the nominal exchange rate. So, for example, if the UK exchange rate falls by 10 per cent then, over a period of years, prices in the UK will rise 10 per cent more than in other countries, causing inflation in the meantime.

Economic growth and the exchange rate

Economic growth and the exchange rate are linked by the effect of competitiveness on international trade (as described in Chapter 2). When the exchange rate appreciates or inflation rises above that of countries with which we trade (ie if the real exchange rate appreciates), exporters find it more difficult to sell goods overseas since the foreign currency price of their goods increases. (Alternatively they may reduce their local currency prices and therefore their profits.) At the same time, imports from overseas become cheaper and overseas producers therefore increase their market share. Both these effects serve to reduce the demand for domestically produced goods and consequently reduce GDP.

Balance of payments and the exchange rate

The balance of payments is affected by both the price and growth effects of movements in the exchange rate. The immediate effect of a fall in the exchange rate is to worsen the balance of payments, even though it increases competitiveness, because it increases the price of imports and decreases the local currency price of exports. In the longer run the general improvement in competitiveness means that the volume of imports decreases while exports increase, thereby overcoming the short-run price effect. This short-run deterioration followed by longer-term improvement of the balance of payments is called the *J-curve effect* (see Figure 6.3).

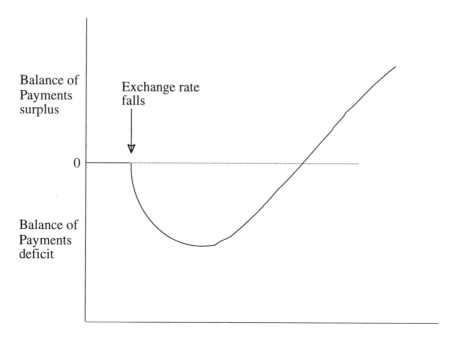

Figure 6.3   *The J-curve*

Macroeconomic influences on the exchange rate

Of course, changes in inflation, trade and growth prospects can also influence the exchange rate. Clearly, if PPP applies, a change in inflation will produce an equal and opposite change in the exchange rate. However, growth and trade patterns can also influence the exchange. The most dramatic example of this is the 'Dutch disease', where the discovery of a natural resource (natural gas in the Netherlands) improves a country's future growth prospects and causes the real exchange rate to appreciate. Unfortunately, although this makes people feel richer (by reducing the price of imports) and allows consumption to increase, it makes other domestic producers' goods more expensive abroad and reduces export volumes (other than those of the natural resource itself). As a result, a country can become solely dependent on the new-found natural resource for export income, and therefore painfully vulnerable to changes in its world price (like many Third World countries); or even to the possibility of its exhaustion.

North Sea oil and the Dutch disease

In the late 1970s the UK's North Sea oil production began to pick up strongly. It became clear that oil would make a major contribution to the UK's balance of trade for many years. As a result, the real exchange rate appreciated sharply, since oil production meant that the UK could keep in trade balance even with a highly uncompetitive exchange rate.

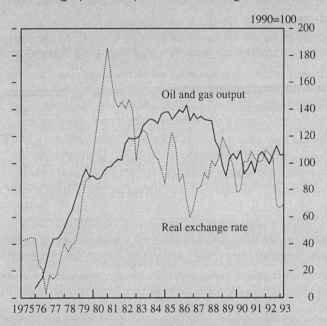

Figure 6.4   *Oil production and the real exchange rate*

Figure 6.4 shows how the UK real exchange rate rose sharply when North Sea oil production came on stream. This reduced the competitiveness of other UK exports.

The main benefit of the strong real exchange rate was that imports were now much cheaper, so that people's standard of living rose and inflation fell. The main cost of the strong real exchange rate was that it became increasingly difficult for non-oil-exporting firms to compete on the world market (or even against imports in the home market). Partly as a result, UK manufacturing industry declined in the early 1980s. The effect is known as the *Dutch disease*, and implies that the consequences of discovering natural resources are not all beneficial, particularly if the natural resource will eventually be exhausted.

Economic policy and the exchange rate

We discussed earlier how movements in the exchange rate can powerfully influence both inflation and growth. It is hardly surprising, therefore, that economic policy in many countries is directed towards control of the exchange rate. Even in countries which do not operate a fixed exchange rate regime, the rate is closely monitored and extreme movements countered by direct policy action.

Monetary and fiscal policy and the exchange rate

Governments can influence the exchange rate most directly through monetary policy. As we saw earlier, relative interest rates exert strong leverage on the exchange rate. Raising interest rates may have a dramatic effect on the exchange rate — causing it to jump to a new level consistent with UIP. However, the jump does not occur if the change in interest rates has been anticipated by the foreign exchange market and incorporated into market expectations.

The link between expectations about monetary policy and the exchange rate implies that indirectly fiscal policy can also play a part through its effect on interest rates. A good example of how the fiscal/monetary policy mix combined to influence the exchange rate was observed in the US during the Reagan administration.

Reaganomics

When President Reagan came to office at the beginning of the 1980s he introduced a radical tax-cutting plan. He felt that US taxes were in the area of the Laffer curve where tax cuts would actually increase revenue (see Chapter 4). He therefore cut taxes in the hope that this would improve the budget deficit. Paul Volker, Chairman of the US Central Bank, the Federal Reserve, was not convinced. He felt that the tax cuts would overheat the economy and cause inflation. As a result, he increased interest rates dramatically just as President Reagan was loosening fiscal policy.

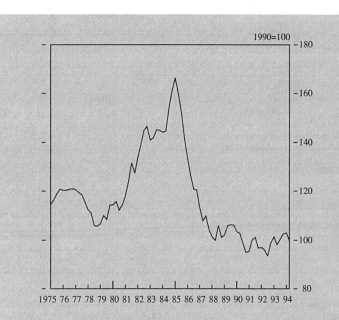

Figure 6.5 *US real exchange rate*

The result of the mixture of loose fiscal and tight monetary policy of the early 1980s was to send the real exchange rate soaring upward, as shown in Figure 6.5, and cause the trade deficit to worsen. As it turned out, Volker was proved to be correct: the government budget deficit increased dramatically and a number of draconian deficit-controlling measures had to be implemented such as the Gramm-Rudman Act, an Act of Congress designed to enforce deficit reduction. Volker's actions had stemmed the inflationary impact of Reagan's measures, but the real exchange rate only came down when deficit control was initiated and concerted action (including intervention by many Central Banks) to bring the dollar down was undertaken in the Louvre Accord of 1984.

Foreign currency intervention

A further source of leverage on the exchange rate is available to governments through foreign currency intervention. Intervention involves buying or selling foreign currency for local currency solely to put pressure on the exchange rate. For example, if a government wishes to support the value of its currency (ie put upward pressure on the exchange rate), it sells foreign currency and purchases its own currency. This artificial increase in the demand for local currency may cause the exchange rate to rise. Governments hold reserves of foreign currency for this purpose, but even if those reserves run to billions of dollars, the turnover in the foreign exchange market shown in Table 6.1 is so huge that foreign exchange intervention can, at best, have only a temporary and marginal effect on the exchange rate.

Fixed vs floating exchange rate regimes

International experience of fixed exchange rate regimes is described in Chapter 8. This section covers the main economic arguments relating to the choice between fixed and floating exchange rate regimes.

As we saw in Chapter 5, credibility is crucial to economic policy. If the government can actually convince people that it is going to pursue a rigid counter-inflation policy, then achieving that policy is facilitated. Chapter 5 also showed that one way of achieving policy credibility was to follow a policy rule which makes it difficult to cheat. ('Cheating', in this case, is defined as loosening policy to generate a short-term pick-up in growth that does not feed through into inflation until much later.) Given that the exchange rate is clearly linked to both inflation and growth, a fixed exchange rate regime, by which the government commits itself to stabilize the exchange rate at a fixed, non-inflationary level, has obvious advantages as a policy rule. Credibility benefits apart, such a policy may also help to encourage trade by reducing the risk of loss for exporting firms in currency transactions. However, such a policy is difficult to implement, for a number of reasons.

Similar policy objectives
Under a fixed exchange rate regime, all the countries in the system are obliged to run similar monetary policies. Theoretically, in a system where absolutely no exchange rate fluctuation is allowed, their interest rates should be identical (refer to the first section of this chapter if it is not clear to you why this should be the case). Furthermore, the loss of absolute control over monetary policy makes it important for the countries in the fixed exchange rate system to have the same policy objectives.

Finding an optimal currency area

A fixed exchange rate regime requires that the country (or countries, in a multicountry system) which you choose to fix against has an economy broadly similar to your own. If not, the constraint of having to run a similar monetary policy will be too onerous. If one country in a fixed exchange rate system suffers a macroeconomic shock (reunification of Germany, for example) which does not directly impinge on other countries, then the burden of implementing the same monetary policy as the affected country (in order to keep the exchange rate fixed) can be unwelcome. If the similarity of the economies concerned is such that a fixed exchange rate regime is preferable to a floating one, those economies are said to form an *optimal currency area*.

Identifying an optimal currency area boils down to establishing where exchange rate adjustment as a means of coping with economic shocks is unnecessary — either because people and capital can move quickly and easily from economically declining areas to booming areas, or because the risk of such macroeconomic events which do not affect the entire area is negligible.

Fixing at the right rate

It must be obvious that, when entering a fixed exchange rate system, it is vital to choose the right exchange rate at which to fix. Ideally, the entry rate should be at, or close to, the PPP rate. Take, for example, a two-country system where the rate chosen differs from the underlying PPP. In that case, one country will quickly tend to experience balance of payments deficits, relatively weak economic growth (as exporters become uncompetitive), and inflation will tend to fall (as a result of weak demand for domestic products in favour of cheaper imports). The other country will experience the opposite effects. Unfortunately, for the reasons we discussed above, establishing valid PPP rates can be very difficult.

Summary

1. Nominal exchange rates are usually defined in terms of bilateral rates (the rate between two countries) or trade-weighted rates. The latter is more important for judging the macroeconomic impact of exchange rate movements.

2. The real exchange rate, which allows for relative inflation between countries, is a measure of competitiveness of a country's goods.

3. Uncovered interest rate parity (UIP) predicts that countries with high interest rates will experience falling exchange rates. However, an unanticipated increase in interest rates will cause the exchange rate to jump upward before falling to its long-run level.

4. In the very long run the real exchange rate will settle at purchasing power parity (PPP) level so that the price of similar goods in different countries is the same.

5. An increase in the real exchange rate will reduce inflation and growth and cause a worsening of the balance of payments in the longer run (although the balance of payments may improve temporarily).

6. Governments attempt to control the exchange rate through monetary policy and foreign currency intervention. The latter, at best, only has a temporary effect.

7. Before deciding whether to fix its exchange rate with another country, a government should look at (a) the credibility benefits of matching economic policy with that of the other country; and (b) the potential trade benefits of an optimal currency area.

Questions for consideration

1. If UK interest rates are 10 per cent and US interest rates are 5 per cent, what change is built into the forward sterling exchange rate over the next year? What might you actually expect to happen to sterling over that period?

2. If UK inflation is 4 per cent and US inflation is 2 per cent, what will happen to the real exchange rate if the nominal exchange rate is unchanged? What effect will this change in the real exchange rate have on UK trade and the balance of payments?

3. If the exchange rate was below PPP, what would you expect to happen to the balance of payments?

4. What would be the likely impact on exports of manufacturing goods if North Sea oil were to run out unexpectedly (think about the exchange rate effect)?

Further reading

Estimates of PPP exchange rates are given in the *OECD Economic Outlook*.

Descriptions of how the foreign exchange market works are given in *Foreign Exchange and Money Market Operations* (Swiss Bank Corporation, 1987) and a more general description of financial markets in *A Random Walk Down Wall Street* (B Malkiel, Norton, 1981).

The US experience under Reagan is described in 'Reaganomics' (O Blanchard, *Economic Policy*, 5, 1987).

7

Monitoring and forecasting the economy

By now you should have a grasp of how growth and inflation vary over the business cycle, and what governments take into account when setting monetary and fiscal policy. In this chapter we show how these concepts are put into practice when monitoring the economy. We describe the indicators which economists use to help judge the current state of activity and the outlook for growth and inflation. Finally, we go beyond the cycle to look at the long-run factors which determine economic performance.

The aim of this chapter is to explain the process of monitoring and forecasting the economy, divided into four steps:

1. How strong is current activity?
2. Where is the economy relative to its potential?
3. What is the outlook for activity?
4. How is policy likely to respond?

How strong is current activity?

The latest GDP figures will provide the most comprehensive picture of current activity, and almost all countries publish these on a quarterly basis. However, the figures are released several weeks after the end of the quarter, so to obtain a more timely picture of activity we need to look at the monthly data releases and survey evidence.

Industrial production figures are available on a monthly basis, although these are also released with a lag of around five or six weeks. For a more current picture we would turn to survey evidence. In the UK both the Confederation of British Industry (CBI) and the Chartered Institute of Purchasing and Supply (CIPS) compile monthly surveys of industrial activity, including questions on current output. These reports run about one month ahead of the official data and give the most timely indication of current industrial activity. The overseas counterparts of the CBI and CIPS surveys are the National Association of Purchasing Managers report in the United States, the Ifo survey in Germany and the INSEE survey in

France. The European Commission regularly publishes the results of surveys from across the European Union.

The main drawback of these surveys, however, is that they only cover production industries, which are around a quarter of national output in most developed economies (see Chapter 2). To some extent this is not a serious problem, as industrial production and national output (GDP) are closely correlated; nevertheless, it is worth supplementing their results with broader surveys where available. For example, in the UK the British Chambers of Commerce (BCC) produce a quarterly survey which covers both manufacturing and service sector firms.

It is also possible to build up a picture of current activity through the expenditure components of GDP — consumption, investment and net trade.

Retail sales figures are the primary source of information on consumer spending. The value and volume of sales are published monthly and cover both food and non-food retailers (which account for about 40 per cent of consumer spending). Another indication of the strength of retail spending is provided by narrow money (notes and coins in circulation, M0 in the UK) which is released ahead of the retail sales figures and moves in line with the level of cash-financed expenditure. The production of consumption goods (published in the industrial production figures) and imports of consumer goods are also good indicators of current consumer spending. Similarly, the level of production and imports of investment goods are a useful measure of fixed capital expenditure.

The contribution of imports and exports to GDP can be largely obtained from the monthly trade figures. Only figures for goods are available on a monthly basis. Data on trade in services is only published quarterly. Nevertheless, as goods account for 85 per cent of total trade they are an accurate indicator of overall imports and exports.

The direction of activity: short term

To gauge the short-term direction of activity (ie over the next three months), we need to look at indicators which provide a slight lead on demand. These are often the more interest-rate-sensitive areas of expenditure, which move in advance of the rest of the economy and are particularly useful when trying to gauge the impact of a change in interest rates. On the consumer side these include new car registrations, consumer credit, and bank and building society mortgage advances. Bank lending figures also provide a further insight into spending, as firms often have to borrow to finance capital expenditure or an increase in stocks. Activity in the construction sector tends to be very interest rate sensitive, so new construction orders and housing starts are also good lead indicators of general activity.

Surveys usually contain information about expected output and future spending plans. For example, in the UK the CBI *Monthly Trends* survey monitors the balance of firms expecting to increase output over the next four months, while the Gallup organization regularly polls households about their financial situation and spending plans.

All of these figures are reported in the press, so it is possible gradually to build up a picture of activity as the quarter progresses. In the box below we give an example of this for the UK using actual figures. Readers wishing to track the economy should try to update this information and supplement it with knowledge of developments in their own industry.

The strength and direction of current activity (UK, January 1995)

Indicator (time period)	% change over 3 months	% change over 12 months
GDP (4th quarter 1994)	0.8	4.0
Manuf output (Sept–Nov)	0.8	5.0
Retail sales (Oct–Dec)	0.5	3.2
Exports (Aug–Oct)	4.5	12.0
Imports (Aug–Oct)	2.0	4.0

Source: Central Statistical Office

Surveys

CBI *Industrial Trends* survey:
  Balance of firms expecting to raise output: Jan +20 (Dec +27)
CIPS Purchasing Managers' index Dec 56.7 (Nov 57.6)

Comment: The economy grew rapidly in the year to the fourth quarter of 1994, with GDP rising 4 per cent. The retail sales figures indicate that consumer spending played an important role in this, with the volume of sales up by more than 3 per cent. However, it is likely that the strongest contribution came from exports, which rose 12 per cent in the three months to October compared with the same period a year ago. This pattern of growth favoured the trade-oriented manufacturing sector which grew by 5 per cent over the year, a better performance than that for the economy as a whole. The figures for the change over three months indicate that the contribution from retail spending is beginning to wane (volumes rose only 0.5 per cent in the fourth quarter), imports are picking up, while exports remain strong. The survey evidence indicates that growth should remain robust but may have weakened slightly — the balance of firms still expect to raise output over the next four months, but the reading was less than in the last CBI survey. Similarly, the Purchasing Managers' index fell back slightly in December.

Where is the economy relative to its potential?

Having determined the strength and direction of current activity, the second step is to find where this puts the economy in relation to its normal or potential output. The concept of potential output and its links with inflation were described in Chapter 3, where we showed that inflation tended to rise when output was above potential and decline when output was below potential. This then allowed us to describe how growth and inflation vary over the cycle.

Clearly, from a corporate planning perspective the best macroeconomic environment for expansion occurs when the economy is below potential and there is the greatest scope for growth without inflation. If activity is above trend it is likely that inflation will soon be rising, if it is not already doing so, and that the authorities will be planning to slow down the economy by raising interest rates.

First, some simple observations. Is inflation falling or rising? The most commonly quoted measure of inflation in the UK is the annual change in the Retail Price Index (RPI). This is calculated monthly by taking the prices of a range of items, from eggs to electricity, and weighting them according to the amount the average consumer spends on them. The RPI index can be thought of as the price of a representative 'basket' of consumer items. The index is important for UK monetary policy as the government is currently aiming to keep the annual change in the RPI index excluding mortgage interest payments (*underlying inflation*) within a 1–4 per cent target band. There are two other measures of inflation which also need to be monitored. The *GDP deflator* is the broadest available measure of inflation as it captures the prices of all the elements of GDP. This is used to 'deflate' nominal GDP to give real GDP in the national accounts, however, as noted above these are released some time after the end of the quarter. The second measure is *manufacturing output prices*, sometimes known as factory gate prices. This information should be supplemented with what you know about the pricing behaviour of your own industry.

If on looking at a variety of measures you conclude that prices and wages have been accelerating over the past year, the economy is likely already to be above potential. This should then be verified by looking at other measures which capture the extent to which resources are being under- or overutilized. Unemployment figures and measures of capacity utilization are both useful for this purpose.

The unemployment rate can be used to judge whether there is slack in the labour market. The level of unemployment should be compared with estimates of its natural rate to determine whether wage pressures are likely to be increasing or decreasing (see Chapter 3). In the UK the natural rate is thought to be around 8 per cent of the workforce. Survey evidence is also useful for judging the state of the labour market; for example, if firms report widespread skill shortages this may be an early sign of inflationary pressure.

Another way of judging available capacity is to look at utilization rates, which are published monthly or quarterly for manufacturing industry in each of the major economies. Figure 7.1 shows the measure for the UK from the CBI *Industrial Trends* survey. The survey asks firms if they are operating below their normal level of capacity. As the number of firms working below normal falls, the amount of spare capacity in industry is reduced. In the figure we have inverted the scale so that as the line rises, capacity utilization increases. Clear cycles can be seen, with capacity utilization forming troughs during the recessions of 1974/75, 1980/81 and 1990/92, and peaks in the boom years of 1972, 1979 and 1988.

These measures should then be compared with empirical estimates of the gap between actual and potential output (the output gap). Most research groups and official bodies regularly publish their own estimates.

In the box below we look at these indicators for the UK.

Where is the economy relative to its potential? (UK, January 1995)

Inflation (y/y %)	% change over year	1 year earlier
GDP deflator (third quarter 1994)	2.2	3.1
Average earnings (Nov)	3.75	3.0
Retail Price Index (Dec): All items	2.9	1.9
RPI excl mortgage interest payments	2.5	2.7
Manufacturing output prices (Dec)	2.6	4.0

Capacity Measures	%	%
Unemployment rate, % workforce (Dec)	8.6	9.9
CBI % below capacity (first quarter 1995)	49	57
Output gap % GDP: OECD (1994)	−3.9	−5.2
Schroders (fourth quarter 1994)	−0.4	−2.0

Sources: Central Statistical Office, CBI, OECD

Comment: Inflation as measured by the GDP deflator has fallen over the past year, indicating that the economy has been operating below its potential. This is supported by estimates of the output gap and figures which show unemployment above its natural rate. However, the output gap is now quite small and the number of firms operating below capacity has fallen, suggesting that there is little slack in the economy and consequently that inflationary pressure may be beginning to build up. The relatively stable rate of underlying inflation (RPI excluding mortgage payments) and the rise in average earnings growth over the past year are signs of this.

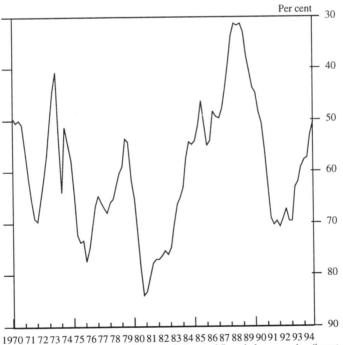

1970 71 72 73 74 75 76 77 78 79 80 81 82 83 84 85 86 87 88 89 90 91 92 93 94
(a) CBI quarterly industrial trends survey, balance of firms below capacity, (inverted).

Figure 7.1 *Capacity utilization*

What is the outlook for activity?

Having identified where the economy is in relation to its potential and the current strength of growth, we are now in a position to consider the outlook for activity. In this section we first look at some longer leading indicators of activity — economic series which can forewarn us of changes in GDP up to 18 months in advance.

Longer leading indicators

Business confidence

Surveys of industry will usually ask business managers if they are more or less optimistic about the future. If they are more confident, it is likely that they are enjoying, or can foresee, an improvement in profitability and are planning an increase in production. Consequently, an increase in business confidence often leads a period of stronger growth.

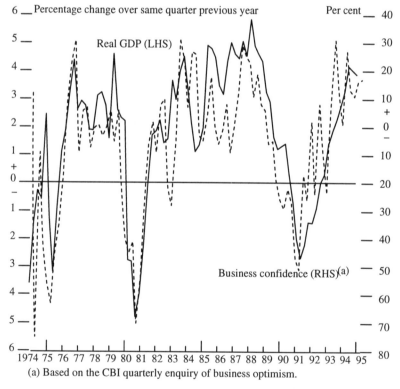

(a) Based on the CBI quarterly enquiry of business optimism.

Figure 7.2   *UK GDP growth and business optimism*

Figure 7.2 shows the close correlation between UK GDP and business confidence as measured by the CBI *Industrial Trends* survey which asks firms if they are more or less optimistic about the future. The confidence series has been pushed forward on the figure by three months to show how it leads GDP growth. This is only representative, and empirical work by the Central Statistical Office (CSO) finds that the lead time varies considerably such that there is an average period of a year between an increase in optimism and above-trend growth. Furthermore, confidence tends to be quite volatile. Part of this reflects seasonality: businesses tend to be confident in the spring and gloomy in the winter. Nevertheless, taking this into account, business confidence is useful for spotting turning points in the economy.

Interest rates

Changes in interest rates affect activity by altering the cost of borrowing, the distribution of income between lenders and borrowers and by influencing the exchange rate (see Chapter 5).

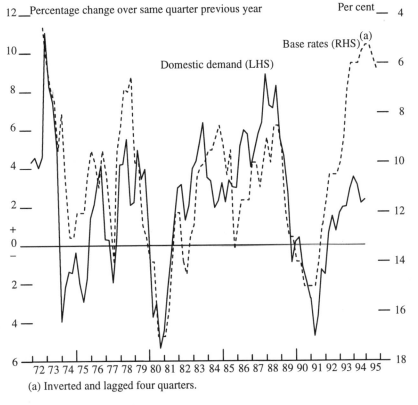

(a) Inverted and lagged four quarters.

Figure 7.3 *Base rate and domestic demand*

In the UK, the relationship between base rates and domestic demand has been quite close. In Figure 7.3 we have pushed the interest rate line forward by nine months to show how it leads changes in GDP, and inverted it so that the correlation between interest rates and activity can be seen more clearly. In recent years the correlation has become looser, with interest rates indicating that domestic demand should be running at around 10 per cent per annum, rather than the 2 per cent pa which has been recorded. There are two reasons for this. First, it is real (ie inflation-adjusted) rather than nominal interest rates which are important for savings and investment decisions (see Chapter 2). Falling inflation has meant that real interest rates have not declined as much as nominal rates in recent years, giving less incentive for households and companies to increase expenditure. Second, having borrowed heavily in the 1980s, firms and households do not wish to take on more debt even though interest rates are low. This aversion to borrowing has muted the impact of lower interest rates.

The yield curve

Another way of judging the impact of interest rates is to compare the current level of short-term rates with their long-term counterparts. The yield curve depicts the different interest rates which can be obtained by investing in bonds of increasing maturity, ie it represents the term structure of interest rates (see Chapter 5). For our purposes it can be represented as the simple difference between long- and short-term interest rates. In each of the major industrial economies, turning points in the differential between long and short rates appear to lead turning points in GDP by about nine months to a year. An upward-sloping yield curve (ie long rates above short) leads stronger GDP growth, while a downward or inverse yield curve has been a leading indicator of weaker economic activity.

An explanation for this lies in the fact that long-term interest rates reflect market expectations of future short rates. Since interest rates are often positively associated with economic activity, an increase in the long rate may reflect the bond markets' expectation of more buoyant future growth. For example, if the government announces that it is cutting taxes, participants in the financial markets will expect stronger growth, which will have to be countered by a higher level of interest rates at some time in the future. Consequently, long-term interest rates will probably rise immediately and the yield curve steepen. To the extent that such expectations are well founded, a steepening of the yield curve should indicate an increase in activity. The opposite argument would hold if long-term rates were to fall below short. In this case the market would be anticipating weaker growth, and therefore cuts in interest rates to support activity.

Figure 7.4 shows the correlation for the US, where we represent the yield curve as the yield on a long-term US government bond minus the interest rate which can be obtained on a three-month deposit. This line has been pushed forward, as with the other leading indicators, to show how it leads changes in GDP.

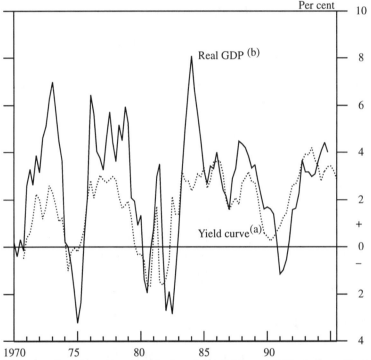

(a) 20 year Government bond yield minus 3 month Treasury bill rate, lagged by 3 quarters.
(b) Percentage change over same quarter previous year.

Figure 7.4 *Yield curve and US GDP*

Money growth

The link between money growth and activity is difficult to assess (see Chapter 5), but three aspects of money make it a useful indicator.

First, some empirical work does show a link between money and activity in many economies. In the UK, for example, there is evidence that both narrow and broad money lead changes in real GDP.

Second, as stronger borrowing acts as one of the key channels from lower interest rates to an increase in activity, the money supply figures provide a useful insight into the effectiveness of monetary policy. An increase in borrowing is reflected in a rise in money growth, as the lender creates a deposit for the borrower to draw on. If interest rates are cut and money growth does not pick up, then demand is likely to remain weak. For example, if the private sector is reluctant to borrow, or banks are reluctant to lend following a period of losses, then money growth will remain weak.

Third, in the long run inflation is a monetary phenomenon. When activity has returned to its potential level, money growth will determine the rate of inflation through the quantity equation described in Chapter 3.

For these reasons most economists monitor the stock of money and lending in the economy.

Summary: Leading indicators

Business confidence, interest rates, the yield curve and money supply are useful for gauging when turning points in activity are in prospect. The average period between a change in one of these indicators and a change in activity is between nine months and a year. However, this can vary considerably and, as we have seen, the correlation can break down, making the indicator less reliable.

In practice, economists will look at a variety of leading indicators (including composite measures), weighting them according to their own prejudices about how the economy works. This will give a general idea of the pace of growth over the next 12 to 18 months. The next step is to take a more detailed look at the individual components of GDP.

Detailed forecasts

To make detailed forecasts economists will usually refer to *econometric equations*, mathematical relationships which describe each component of GDP in terms of its key determinants. These equations are estimated using statistical techniques which produce the 'line of best fit' over a period of time with the actual series. For example, the consumer spending equation will contain terms for real income, wealth and interest rates, where the weights on each are estimated so that the equation gives the best prediction of actual consumer spending in the past. The equation will also be tested to ensure that it does not consistently over- or underestimate actual consumption.

Econometric equations may be used individually, or as part of a model which determines total GDP and allows for the interactions between growth and inflation. Some larger models contain over 50 key equations which, when fed with some assumptions about interest rates and fiscal policy, will produce full-scale macroeconomic forecasts. There was a time when macroeconometric models were thought to be the best method of forecasting the economy. Econometric methods meant that economic theories could be tested in a scientific way to develop an accurate representation of the real economy. The model could also take into account the different interactions and feedbacks between growth and inflation. However, in recent years the forecasting record of large-scale macro models has been disappointing. For example, between June 1990 and December 1992 forecasters at the OECD in Paris consistently predicted a recovery in world output which failed to materialize. Similar errors were made by other forecasting groups. This has led to a reappraisal of large macro models, and economists are now far more sceptical about the forecasts they produce.

The problem for the econometric models is that their predictions about the future are only reliable if the patterns of the past repeat themselves. Because economics is not a physical science, these relationships, say between consumer spending and interest rates, are not cast in stone. Consequently, the parameters on which the models are based can alter and undermine the results they produce. Nevertheless, the models do provide a useful discipline. They enable us to look at the key determinants of aggregate demand in a structured way and, when combined with a view of how the world may have changed since the model was estimated, provide a framework for forecasts.

We do not intend to describe a full macro model of activity, but instead concentrate on the key determinants of aggregate demand as described in Chapter 2. The aim is to provide a brief guide to the main influences on demand so that the reader can assess the forecasts produced by the macro models.

Consumer spending
To forecast consumer spending we need to estimate the likely growth in real disposable income and then subtract (or add) any increase (decrease) in savings.

Real income growth A rough estimate of real income can be obtained by taking the difference between wage growth and inflation over the forecast period and adjusting for any increase in unemployment. In practice this means making a projection of nominal wage growth from recent pay settlements (adding in an element for bonuses) and then subtracting an estimate of inflation. (This estimate

may have to be changed when we have looked more closely at inflation prospects, but it provides a starting point.) If tax increases are
planned or expected, they should also be deducted from disposable
income. To gauge the likely change in unemployment we would look
at recent trends in employment and surveys of firms' employment
intentions.

Savings
1. *Wealth*. Savings are determined by real wealth and real interest
    rates (see Chapter 2). Therefore the forecast should contain a
    view on how asset prices (particularly house prices) and inter-
    est rates are likely to change. The house-price income ratio
    provides a guide to whether houses are under- or overvalued
    (see Figure 7.5), with the scope for a rise in house prices at its
    greatest when the ratio is low. We would supplement this with
    other measures of affordability from the Council of Mortgage
    lenders.

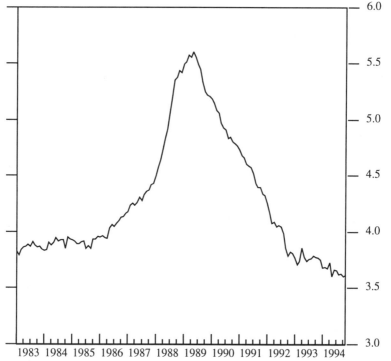

(a) Halifax house price index divided by the Department of Employment 's seasonally
adjusted measure of whole economy earnings.

Figure 7.5   *House-price income ratio*

2. *Interest rates*. Judging the course of interest rates is an end in itself, as it is a major determinant of the performance of bond and equity markets. Most forecasts will take the path of interest rates implied by the yield curve as a starting point. This then enables us to determine where the economy is heading on the assumptions which are discounted by the financial markets. In the final section of this chapter we review these policy settings to decide whether the government is likely to respond differently in the light of the forecast.

These are the main influences on consumer spending. To quantify them we would refer to an econometric equation. The results would then be adjusted in the light of its recent forecasting performance and our own views on any factors which are not being fully picked up.

Investment and stockbuilding

In Chapter 2 we highlighted the influences on investment and stock-building as expected demand, capacity constraints, company finances and interest rates.

Expected demand and capacity constraints Business surveys are usually the best source of information on corporate expectations of demand and capacity constraints. We have already referred to the CBI survey for the UK, and would compare this with other surveys such as that issued quarterly by the Chambers of Commerce which includes service sector companies.

Company finances Information on the state of company finances is available from a number of sources. Gross trading profits and the financial balance of industrial and commercial companies are pub-lished by the CSO, which also produces information on the balance sheet of the sector. For more timely data on the liquidity of the cor-porate sector, see the sectoral money supply figures which are published quarterly by the Bank of England.

Exports and Imports

Imports are primarily determined by domestic demand and com-petitiveness (see Chapter 2), with capacity utilization also playing a role when the economy rises significantly beyond its ability to sup-ply (see Chapter 3). For exports the same influences are important, except that it is world rather than domestic demand which is the driving force.

Domestic demand An estimate of domestic demand should be available from the above analysis of consumption and investment expenditure, and for capacity utilization we would use the CBI survey measure also quoted above.

World demand World demand can be determined from forecasts for domestic demand in the country's trading partners. These should then be weighted by the relative size of each export market (see Figure 2.).

Competitiveness There is no single measure of competitiveness, but for forecasting purposes economists tend to concentrate on the relative cost or price of domestic goods, compared with their overseas counterparts. One of the most commonly used measures is the IMF index of relative unit labour costs. This compares unit labour costs in the home country against a trade-weighted basket of unit labour costs in its trading partners, adjusted into a common currency. If costs at home are increasing faster than those overseas (either due to higher inflation or a rise in the exchange rate), exporters will find it harder to keep their prices in line with their competitors in international markets. This is then likely to lead to a loss of market share, so that exports do not rise as quickly as world demand. For an initial forecast of the exchange rate we would use the values implied by forward market rates (see Chapter 6).

Bringing in the supply side

The above analysis enables us to build up a picture of aggregate demand from each of the components of expenditure. To turn this into a forecast for GDP, we must now consider the ability of the economy to meet any increase in demand. If the economy is starting from a point where it is close to potential, then stronger demand may result in higher price inflation, rather than an increase in output. To assess this we need to combine our earlier estimate of initial spare capacity with a forecast of the growth in potential supply.

Estimating potential output growth

In Chapter 3 we described how the potential output of an economy will depend on the growth in its labour force, the increase in its capital stock and a third factor known as total factor productivity. We then showed how, on a relatively simple assumption about the relationship between output, labour and capital, UK potential output could be projected to rise at 2.4 per cent over the next five years. If, for example, the economy were then thought to be 1 per cent below potential, there is scope for aggregate demand to rise at 3 per cent per annum for two years before potential is reached. Consequently, the increase in actual GDP will be close to aggregate demand.

If, on the other hand, activity was expected to rise above potential, we would have to reduce our forecasts for real GDP growth. Part of the increase in demand will be met by working capacity harder, but some will be lost, either because firms will raise prices and choke off demand, or because extra imports come in to meet demand. This would be reflected in our forecasts by trimming consumption, as higher inflation reduces real incomes and household spending power, and by raising imports as a share of domestic demand.

In addition to this we also need to look at cost pressures on the price level. If unit labour costs or other input prices are increasing rapidly, then firms will try to pass these onto their customers to maintain profitability. An output gap will dampen this effect, but nevertheless there could still be some upward pressure on prices. Similarly, strong money growth could push up inflation in the long run through the quantity equation (see Chapters 3 and 5).

To give the reader an idea of how these factors are incorporated into an actual forecast, we have set out the key elements of a recent forecast for the UK in the box below.

UK Growth Forecast

% change on year earlier	1994	1995	1996
Consumer spending	2.3	1.6	2.4
Real disposable income	-0.1	1.5	2.6
Base interest rate (%)	5.5	7.3	7.9
House prices	0.4	2.4	3.6
Fixed investment	3.5	5.2	5.0
Corporate profits	18.1	7.6	3.2
Capacity utilization	17.5	25.5	29.0
Stockbuilding (% GDP)	0.5	0.4	-0.1
Government consumption	1.7	0.7	0.5
Exports	8.7	7.8	5.1
World demand	7.3	8.3	6.3
Trade-weighted exchange	0.1	-1.9	-0.8
Imports	5.4	5.0	4.3
Domestic demand	2.9	2.4	2.4
Gross Domestic Product	3.8	3.2	2.6

Comment: GDP growth is expected to slow in 1995 and 1996 as consumer spending and export growth ease back, while stock-building makes less of a contribution. In 1994 consumer spending outpaced real income as the personal sector ran down its savings; however over the next two years rising interest rates and a weak recovery in house prices are expected to encourage households to maintain their savings and consumption only rises in line with income. In the corporate sector rising profits and increasing capacity utilization stimulate an increase in fixed capital investment. On the trade side, strong growth in world demand supports robust export growth.

Source: Ernst & Young ITEM Club, Winter 1994

Inflation Outlook

% change on year earlier	1994	1995	1996
Output gap (% GDP)	−2.0	−0.0	0.5
Unit labour costs	0.3	1.1	1.9
Import prices	0.8	0.1	2.7
RPI (excl. mortgage payments)	2.4	2.5	2.8

Comment: Inflation is expected to stabilize in 1995 as the output gap closes. In 1996 the economy is expected to rise above trend (see output gap) and, with unit labour costs and import prices rising, inflation is expected to rise.

How is policy likely to respond?

In the previous section we used as starting assumptions the path of interest rates which is discounted by the markets, and the exchange rate which is consistent with interest parity. Tax rates and public expenditures are projected on the basis of government plans, usually announced at budget time. We refer to this as the *base forecast*.

Once a projection has been produced on this basis we have to ask if the government and financial markets would be happy with the outcome and, if not, whether the course of monetary and fiscal policy would be different. There are three key areas which could prompt a policy response.

The first and most obvious is inflation. If inflation is accelerating then the government will have to raise interest rates to cool activity and bring the economy back toward its potential. After the 1970s when inflation wreaked havoc in the industrial economies, most

countries adopted an anti-inflation stance. The objective of monetary policy in most countries today is to ensure that inflation
remains under control. In the UK the government has an explicit
target of 1–4 per cent for underlying inflation, while in countries
such as Germany and New Zealand the central bank is required to
maintain the stability of the price level. Sharp rises in inflation
should prompt an increase in interest rates which should be incorporated into the forecast. If no such policy response were
forthcoming, it would seem reasonable to assume a fall in the
exchange rate as financial markets would lose confidence in the
government's willingness to control inflation and, fearing a loss of
competitiveness, would sell the currency.

The second area is the balance of payments. In the international
capital markets it is possible for one country to run a balance of payments deficit for some time. Indeed, if an economy is developing
rapidly it may be expected to run a balance of payments deficit as it
imports the capital goods which are needed to generate future
exports. However, a deteriorating trade deficit could either signal
that the economy is overheating or that it has become uncompetitive. We looked at these scenarios in Chapter 3.

In the case of overheating, the deterioration in trade would be due
to a sharp rise in imports, as home producers have reached the limits of their capacity and domestic demand is increasingly met from
overseas. The appropriate policy response would be a rise in interest rates or a tightening of fiscal policy to reduce domestic demand
and cut imports. Signs that the economy has become uncompetitive
would be if imports were rising significantly even though domestic
demand was weak, and/or exports were not responding to an
increase in world demand. In this case economic growth would be
subdued even though demand was relatively strong, and it may be
necessary to allow the currency to fall to restore competitiveness.
However, such action is only likely to succeed in the short run:
unless the underlying causes of the lack of competitiveness are tack-
led (such as high inflation, poor productivity) the problem will soon
return.

The third trouble spot is the Public Sector Borrowing Requirement
(PSBR), the difference between government receipts and expenditure. To finance its borrowing the government will issue bonds
which add to its stock of outstanding debt (see Chapter 4). The ser-
vicing of this debt then adds to future interest payments, placing a
burden on future budgets. If the PSBR is deteriorating rapidly then it
is possible for the government to fall into a 'debt trap' where interest
payments absorb an ever-increasing proportion of government

expenditure and debt as a share of GDP rises inexorably. Therefore, the implications of the forecast for the government finances need to be checked to ensure that borrowing is on a sustainable path. If debt is on an ever upward trend then taxes will have to be raised or public expenditure cut to restore stability. Clearly, this would have adverse implications for domestic demand and growth which would need to be factored into the forecast.

Medium-term prospects

The steps we have described should enable you to gain a picture of where the economy is at present and where it is heading over the next two to three years. Such a time horizon is often sufficient for most of a company's operations. Sometimes, however, management needs to take a longer view. For example, where large-scale capital projects are involved the firm will be interested in demand over the next 10 or 20 years. Time horizons of this length are common for infrastructure projects; for example, it may take two years to build a power station or road which is then expected to have an operating life of around 20 years. Projections of this duration are subject to an even wider margin of error than the relatively short-term forecasts described above. Nevertheless, the firm must have some idea of likely demand if it is to assess the feasibility of a project. In these circumstances the firm will test the viability of a project on a number of different scenarios around a central projection. Only if the project is viable on a number of possible outcomes is it likely to proceed.

The basic guiding principle in this type of analysis is that in the long run the economy can only grow in line with potential output. As we have seen, if activity is persistently above potential, resources will be strained, inflation will accelerate and money will rapidly lose its value. This will steadily undermine competitiveness until policy is tightened to bring GDP back toward potential. Conversely, if activity is below potential, resources will be underutilized, and as inflation is not a threat the government will stimulate activity to reduce unemployment. Therefore, medium-term forecasts are effectively projections of aggregate supply, and we would follow the principles outlined in Chapter 3 on estimating supply. Different scenarios can be constructed to reflect different assumptions about labour force growth, the increase in capital stock and total factor productivity.

Summary

1. The process of monitoring and forecasting the economy begins with looking at figures for GDP, industrial production and retail sales to gauge the strength of current activity. We would then look at surveys of industry and households to determine whether the pace of activity is likely to be maintained in the near future.

2. The next step is to decide whether the economy is above or below its potential (ie is there an output gap?). Signs of pressure on resources may already be apparent in prices and wages, but any conclusions should be verified by looking at the level of unemployment and capacity utilization. You should also check direct estimates of the output gap which are often published by the main research groups.

3. To judge the outlook for activity we would first look at leading indicators such as business confidence, interest rates, the yield curve and money growth. To make a detailed projection we would forecast the individual expenditure components of GDP, based on their key determinants. This will give us a projection for the rise in aggregate demand.

4. To turn this into a forecast for real GDP we need to consider whether the economy has the resources to meet an increase in expenditure. Our estimate of the output gap will tell us how much slack there is at present, and to judge future capacity we make an estimate of the likely growth in potential output.

5. If demand is then likely to exceed supply, our forecast for real GDP needs to be reduced to allow for an increase in inflation and rise in imports.

6. Finally, we need to consider the likely policy response from the authorities. If inflation were expected to rise or the balance of payments significantly deteriorate, our forecast should allow for an increase in interest rates. Similarly, if the government finances were expected to deteriorate significantly we may need to factor in a tightening of fiscal policy.

7. These steps should enable you to gain an idea of where the economy is now and where it is heading over the next two to three years. For longer forecast horizons we would look at projections of potential output, as this determines the sustainable level of production over the medium term.

Action steps

1. You should now be in a position to follow the economy. While you may not wish to produce full economic forecasts, you should have an idea of where the economy is in its cycle and the next move in interest rates. To keep track of recent events try updating the tables in this chapter with the latest economic figures which are usually published in the press. Then look out for forecasts from the main economic institutes and the government (see further reading below).
2. How do the forecasts produced for the economy square with experience in your industry? Compare your sales and orders with the latest projections for the whole economy. By doing this you can gain a 'feel' for whether your business tends to perform in line with the overall economy, a little ahead or lagging behind. You may then be able to develop your own leading indicators from information collected by your industry.

Further reading

Data sources and surveys

Most of the information required to follow the UK economy can be found in *Economic Trends* (published monthly by the Central Statistical Office). A useful summary of recent developments is the *Monthly Monetary Report* produced by HM Treasury. Surveys to watch out for are the Confederation of British Industry's *Monthly Trends Enquiry*, its *Quarterly Industrial Trends* survey and its monthly *Wholesale and Distributive Trades* survey. The Chartered Institute of Purchasing and Supply publishes a monthly survey, and the British Chambers of Commerce publish a quarterly survey.

Official reports on the UK

The Inflation Report is released by the Bank of England with its *Quarterly Bulletin*. An analysis of the economy is contained in *The Financial Statement and Budget Report* published by HM Treasury. The Treasury also publishes *The Report of the Independent Panel of Forecasters*, analysis and forecasts from the 'wise men'.

Regular forecasts (UK and world)

For a comprehensive analysis of economic trends and the outlook for the world economy, see the *OECD Economic Outlook* and the *IMF World Outlook*. Forecasts and analysis can also be found in the *London Business School Economic Outlook* and the *National Institute Economic Review*. For a monthly summary of forecasts see *Consensus Forecasts*.

8

Current issues in macroeconomics

The aim of this chapter is to apply some of the concepts to which you have been exposed so far to two important macroeconomic phenomena:

1. the history of fixed exchange rate regimes, including the European Exchange Rate Mechanism (ERM);
2. the rise in unemployment since the 1970s.

Fixed exchange rate regimes and the ERM

In Chapter 6 we saw how a fixed exchange rate regime can both encourage trade and provide a simple and credible framework for monetary policy. Chapter 6 also discussed the conditions required for a successful fixed exchange rate regime, including the requirement for there to be similar economies and similar policy objectives between members. This chapter looks at the history of the ERM and previous exchange rate regimes and, although it does not answer the question as to whether European Monetary Union is feasible, it offers historical evidence which you may use to form your own judgement.

History of fixed exchange rate regimes before the ERM

The Gold Standard

In 1879, following the demise of bimetallism (in which both gold and silver were used to back paper currencies), the Gold Standard was taken up by the major economies. The Gold Standard acted as a fixed exchange rate regime, because each country's paper currency was convertible into gold at a fixed rate which implicitly meant that every currency involved was convertible into another currency at a fixed rate via gold. The Gold Standard was intended to work by requiring a country's paper currency to be 100 per cent backed by gold reserves. In practice, however, many countries operated a system whereby only a relatively small proportion of their currencies was fully backed. For example, by the late nineteenth century the Bank of England was employing a system in which only 30–50 per cent of the currency was covered by gold reserves.

Even so, the Gold Standard provided a reliable automatic mechanism controlling both inflation and trade imbalances. Inflation was decisively controlled by the limit on the total available supply of gold, and interest rates rose naturally as a response to inflationary pressure (such as an increase in aggregate demand). In other words, since the total supply of money was determined by the supply of gold, an increase in the demand for money without a corresponding increase in the supply of gold merely generated higher interest rates (this relationship follows from the link between the demand for base money and interest rates described in Chapter 5). A similar mechanism ensured that trade imbalances between countries would also be automatically removed. Any country with a current account deficit was obliged physically to export gold (to pay for the excess of imports over exports). Its money supply would thereby be reduced — producing higher interest rates, reduced import demand and consequently an eventual improvement in its balance of payments.

The automaticity of the Gold Standard had two major benefits:

1. *Low inflation*. Since governments could not use monetary policy to gain a short-term boost to output, average inflation was quite low.
2. *Trade stability*. Gold acted as a single common currency for trade between the major countries and prevented large trade imbalances.

However, automaticity also had two major disadvantages:

1. *Volatile inflation*. Although the Gold Standard period was characterized by low average inflation, individual country inflation was highly sensitive to external factors such as new discoveries of gold and the hoarding of gold. These external factors created substantial distortions in the overall money supply and hence inflation levels. In particular, there were a number of periods in which UK prices fell quite dramatically, as Figure 8.1 shows.
2. *Volatile output*. Output and therefore employment were highly variable because governments were powerless to adjust monetary policy to local economic conditions.

Figure 8.1 shows average annual RPI inflation rates over the Gold Standard period. Although inflation tended to be low, it was highly variable, with many periods of falling prices.

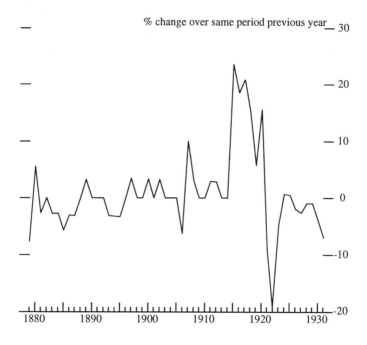

Figure 8.1   *UK inflation over the Gold Standard*

The most dramatic demonstration of the problems involved occurred after the First World War when the UK (under the Chancellorship of Winston Churchill) decided to re-enter the Gold Standard (suspended in Europe over the war years) at the pre-war parity. Unfortunately, UK prices had doubled during the war while the US had maintained its Gold Standard parity throughout. Returning at the pre-war gold/sterling parity therefore meant that sterling was grossly overvalued and the real exchange rate could only be reduced by a deep recession and falling prices. UK unemployment was therefore already high even before the Great Depression struck in the early 1930s. The depression further increased the pressure on the UK economy and in 1931 sterling was allowed to float, signalling the end of the Gold Standard era.

The Bretton Woods exchange rate system
After the demise of the Gold Standard, a number of countries began to devalue their currencies very rapidly. They felt that this would stimulate their own economies at the expense of others and thus avoid the worst effects of the depression. There followed a round of competitive devaluations with countries seeking to cut their exchange rates more rapidly than their trading partners. Described

as 'beggar-thy-neighbour', this policy was widely pursued between 1931 and 1939, a period characterized by rapidly falling and extremely volatile exchange rates.

After the Second World War, a major international conference was convened at Bretton Woods (a ski resort in New Hampshire, USA). The conference objective was to restore order to the international monetary system following the war and the turmoil of the post-Gold Standard period. The conference set up a system of fixed exchange rates with the International Monetary Fund (IMF) as the watchdog, both to ensure that there were no competitive devaluations and to offer loans to countries with short-term balance of payments problems. Notionally, the Bretton Woods system was a new form of Gold Standard with each currency keeping its exchange rate within a 1 per cent band of fluctuation around a par value with gold. However, as a direct result of the Second World War, the US held about 70 per cent of the world's gold reserves, and therefore the new system effectively implied fixed parities against the dollar. Certainly, the dollar became the main trading and reserve currency, and the dollar-based Bretton Woods system was accordingly faced with two main problems:

1. *Ensuring the supply of dollars.* Since all countries required dollars both for trading purposes and as a reserve currency, the US was obliged to run a continuing balance of payments deficit in order to provide dollars to the rest of the world. Inevitably these continuing deficits reduced confidence in the dollar, and made it clear that even the huge US gold reserves were not sufficient to cover the international demand for dollars.

2. *Seigniorage income.* The enormous international demand for dollars also enabled the US to print more money for a given rate of inflation than was possible for others. Effectively, the system meant that other countries were giving an interest-free loan to the US (and so helping to fund its deficits). Many countries resented giving the US this advantage.

Although the Bretton Woods system operated effectively until the mid-1960s, US spending (particularly on the Vietnam War) led to ever-increasing US deficits which many countries were unwilling to fund. In the mid-1960s, France made a strong public gesture by swapping its dollar reserves for gold. This action and the consequent market reaction forced other countries in the system to sell large quantities of gold to keep the underlying par value unchanged. Increasing pressure was thereby imposed on the system and in 1971 President Nixon suspended the dollar/gold parity — thus ending the Bretton Woods arrangement.

The rise and fall of the ERM

The ERM (Exchange Rate Mechanism) of the EMS (European Monetary System) was formally set up in 1978. In practice it was largely an adaptation of the 'snake' arrangement which had operated after the end of the Bretton Woods system. All nine of the countries then in the EC joined the EMS, but the UK postponed its entry into the ERM (the fixed exchange rate regime). In the event, the UK did not join the ERM until 1990.

What are the rules of the ERM system?

The ERM is based on a system of fixed but adjustable exchange rates. There is a fixed official parity between each pair of currencies which gives a *parity grid* for all the currencies in the ERM. However, each currency is allowed a margin of fluctuation around the official parity and can, in extreme circumstances, negotiate a new parity. The margin of fluctuation allowed also varies; most countries operated within a 2.25 per cent margin (called the narrow band) up until 1993, although Spain, Portugal and the UK operated within 6 per cent margins (wide bands). Since then, those countries which remain in the ERM have used 15 per cent margins.

To keep within the allowed margins of fluctuation, member country governments undertake to make their monetary policy consistent with their parity and to intervene in the foreign exchange market if and when necessary (see Chapter 6 for details on currency intervention). To ensure that member countries can intervene in strength, the ERM has an automatic borrowing system called the Very Short Term Financing Facility (VSTF), which allows member countries to borrow almost unlimited amounts of foreign exchange from other member countries at short notice.

As we have seen, the Bretton Woods system perished largely because the dollar acquired a special international status. The ERM sought to avoid this problem by the creation of the stateless European Currency Unit (ECU) in the central currency role. The ECU was defined as a weighted average of all the currencies in the EMS. As the ERM system progressed, however, it became clear that the central currency role was being taken over by the Deutschmark, because not only was it the most important single currency in the ECU, but other member countries sought to align themselves closely with the monetary policy of the German Bundesbank. By so doing, they aimed to acquire the monetary policy credibility of the Bundesbank.

Through the leadership of the Bundesbank the ERM formulated two objectives:

1. To ensure exchange rate stability both to encourage trade in the EC and to prepare the European economy for a single currency.
2. To encourage all ERM countries to converge on Germany's low inflation performance.

Convergence on German economic performance became implicit in the terms of ERM membership. A country trying to fix its exchange rate against the DM was obliged to follow Germany's monetary policy line, which, as the system leader, was based on German domestic considerations. Figure 8.2 illustrates how the major ERM member countries' interest rates tended to move in line with those in Germany. Another interesting feature emerging from the figure is that interest rates in the other major ERM countries were always higher than those in Germany. Other ERM countries were always more likely to realign their exchange rate downwards against Germany rather than upwards – a risk for which the foreign exchange markets needed to be compensated by higher interest rates (as explained in Chapter 6). The margin between German and other interest rates narrowed over the 1980s because the risk of exchange rate realignment diminished (see Figure 8.3).

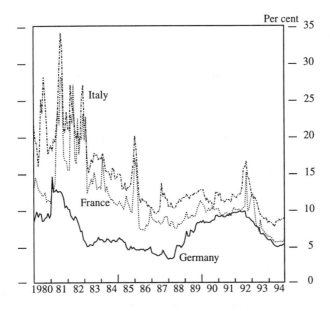

Figure 8.2 *Interest rates in the ERM countries*

Figure 8.3   *ERM exchange rates (against the DM)*

The history of the ERM

How well did the ERM achieve the two aims defined above? Figure 8.3 shows the exchange rates of some ERM member countries against the DM since the beginning of the ERM, and reveals how, over the 1980s, the ERM led to increasingly stable exchange rates (the UK, which joined quite late, experienced far more exchange rate volatility against the DM than did France and Italy). During the early years of the ERM, there were many realignments as countries attempted to find the optimum exchange rates and prevent their real exchange rates from getting too far out of line. In the late 1980s, parities grew increasingly rigid as the economic performance of the member countries became more similar. Inflation rates in the ERM countries also converged over the 1980s with German levels and so, in that decade at least, the ERM seemed to be very successful in achieving the twin aims of stable exchange rates and inflation convergence. The disappointing aspect of this period was that the reductions in inflation achieved were at the cost of high unemployment and low growth. This was particularly disappointing because many countries felt that, by linking their economies to Germany, they would instantly acquire Germany's credibility and the process of reducing inflation would therefore be much less painful.

Given the relative success of the ERM during the 1980s, what went wrong in the 1990s? As Figure 8.3 shows, the ERM went through two crises. The first was in October 1992 when Italy and the UK were forced out of the ERM system. The second was in September 1993 when all the remaining ERM countries (except the Netherlands) were obliged to accept much wider 15 per cent bands of fluctuation, which effectively meant that the ERM was no longer operative. There were a number of factors behind the ERM crisis:

1. *Increased real exchange rate divergence.* Although there was substantial convergence of inflation rates over the 1980s, the differentials between Germany and some other ERM countries (Italy in particular) meant that maintaining fixed nominal exchange rates implied that real exchange rates were moving further and further out of line. In the early 1980s, this problem had been overcome by fairly frequent realignments but, as the ERM parities became increasingly rigid, the problem worsened. The UK, in particular, suffered from this situation. Having entered the ERM quite late (when realignments were rare), the UK did not have the option of realignment to deal with any real exchange rate problems.

2. *Doubts about EMU.* The foreign exchange markets were convinced that the ERM member countries were committed to keeping their ERM parities as an important step towards the single currency proposal underlying European Monetary Union (EMU). In 1992, increased doubts were expressed about EC commitment to EMU (in particular, a referendum in Denmark rejected EMU) and this development also cast doubt on the ERM itself.

3. *German reunification.* In 1990 East and West Germany were reunited, representing a major economic upheaval for Germany. The set-up of the ERM, however, meant that all the ERM countries had to continue to follow German monetary policy and implement policies consistent with acute economic conditions which only the system leader was actually experiencing. Accordingly, it became clear that all the ERM countries except Germany were being forced to maintain interest rates much higher than they would have wished. The foreign exchange market soon realized and reacted to this development.

Following two periods of exchange rate turbulence in 1992 and 1993, the ERM effectively came to an end. Most EU countries still operate within 15 per cent fluctuation bands, but this can hardly be called a fixed exchange rate regime. European Monetary Union (EMU) in which all EU countries employ a common currency is, however, still the stated objective.

Unemployment

Probably the greatest failure of macroeconomics is its inability to find remedies for, or even satisfactorily explain, the very high natural rate of unemployment experienced by many countries over the last 20 years. Standard economic theory would predict that all available economic resources will be used at the going market price, ie that supply and demand will be equal at the market price. However, in many countries we observe the phenomenon of *involuntary unemployment*, where there are large numbers of people who are willing to supply labour at the current market wage (or even below the current market wage) but find that there is no demand.

Table 8.1   *Unemployment rates in 1970 and 1990*

	1970 (%)	1990 (%)
Canada	5.6	8.1
France	2.5	8.9
Germany	0.8	5.0
Italy	3.8	7.9
Japan	1.1	2.1
UK	3.0	6.5
USA	4.8	5.5

Source: *Unemployment* (Layard, R, Jackman R, and Nickell, S)

As Table 8.1 shows, unemployment rates were relatively low and similar across the seven major economies in 1970. However, in the 1970s and 1980s a number of countries experienced a dramatic increase in unemployment rates which has persisted into the 1990s. It seems that the deep recessions following the two oil price rises in 1973 and 1979 were mainly responsible for the rise in unemployment, but why did it stay so high? And why did unemployment rise in some countries but not in others? A number of explanations have been put forward.

Wage determination

Following the rise in oil prices, most governments attempted to reduce the consequent inflation by restricting demand growth. In order for this not to lead to higher unemployment, wage growth had to fall dramatically through a flexible system of wage determination. It seems that this flexibility was present in countries with either highly centralized national-level or decentralized company-level wage-bargaining systems, but not in intermediate industry-level systems. The reason may be that at both company level and national level, wage negotiators can observe the employment and output consequences of their actions. Excessive wage growth at a company level may cause the firm to go out of business, and at national level it may simply cause further inflation. At industry level, however, it may be possible to achieve real wage growth at the expense of other industries or other groups in the same industry. Examples of highly centralized wage-bargaining systems include those of Sweden, Norway and Austria, while the USA has a highly decentralized system.

Successful centralized wage-bargaining systems are also highly unionized. This suggests that it is not the existence of trade unions but the nature of the bargaining structure which is responsible for inflexible labour markets.

The benefit system

There are two aspects of the unemployment benefit system that contribute to persistently high levels of unemployment: the level of benefit, and its duration.

The most significant aspect of the level of benefit is the *replacement ratio*. This measures the value of unemployment benefit as a proportion of the wage an unemployed person could, on average, expect to earn if he or she found employment. The replacement ratio is important simply because it quantifies the potential improvement in living standards of an unemployed person who finds a job. If the ratio is very high (ie the value of unemployment benefit is similar to the expected wage), then an unemployed person has little incentive to try to find work.

However, most research has found that the duration of benefit is possibly even more important than the replacement ratio. The outstanding feature of the rise in unemployment in the 1970s and 1980s was the increase in the average length of time spent unemployed, as opposed to the increase in the number of people becoming unemployed. Many argue that it was this phenomenon which explains why unemployment did not fall back when the world economy recovered. They suggest that the long-term unemployed (those unemployed for over a year) are different from other unemployed in that it is more difficult for them to re-enter the labour market. There are two reasons:

Table 8.2 *Unemployment and unemployment benefit regimes*

	Unemployment rate 1983–8 average	Long-term unemployed % of total	Duration of benefit (years)	Replacement ratio %	Expenditure on employment programmes per unemployed (as % of output per head)
Canada	9.9	7	0.5	60	4.3
France	9.9	45	3.75	57	3.9
Germany	6.7	47	indefinite	63	10.4
Italy	7.0	69	0.5	2	0.8
Japan	2.7	21	0.5	60	5.6
UK	10.7	45	indefinite	36	4.6
USA	7.1	7	0.5	50	2.4
Norway	2.7	6	1.5	65	9.8
Sweden	2.2	8	1.2	80	34.6

Source: *Unemployment* (Layard, Jackman and Nickell)

they may have given up looking for work, and/or employers may find them less employable (employers may ask themselves why nobody has given them a job before). The argument suggests that policies directed at reducing long-term unemployment may be the most successful way of reducing total unemployment without putting upward pressure on wages. There are two policies available: either to withdraw benefit after a period, thereby forcing the unemployed to accept virtually any job; or to engage in active labour market policies and try to train or find jobs for the long-term unemployed. The US offers an example of the first approach, while the Nordic countries and Austria have followed the second. Table 8.2 above shows how different countries have pursued different benefit and training policies and their relative success in reducing unemployment.

Labour market mismatch

Those currently seeking employment may not match up with firms seeking employees because of the following:

1. *Regional mismatch*. If the unemployed are concentrated in one region while employment growth is in another, the regional unemployed are effectively excluded from the labour market and the natural rate of unemployment for the economy as a whole will be higher. Although one would expect that over the medium term either firms would move toward the cheaper labour or the labour would move towards the jobs, some regional disparities in unemployment (such as between northern and southern Italy) have proved to be remarkably persistent.
2. *Skills mismatch*. Estimates for Britain and the US suggest that the unemployment rate for semi-skilled and unskilled workers is over four times higher than that for professional and managerial workers. Unemployment rates also differ significantly between industries.
3. *Demographic mismatch*. As Table 8.3 shows, unemployment rates can vary quite substantially by age, race and sex.

Although mismatch is important in determining the level of unemployment, it was not responsible for the rapid rise in unemployment in the 1970s and 1980s. Contrary to popular belief, skills mismatch through rapid industrial change is no more common now than it was in the 1950s and 1960s when large numbers of people moved from the agricultural to the manufacturing sector.

Some combination of the factors described in the section may help explain the persistently high levels of unemployment experienced by

Table 8.3   *Unemployment by age, race and sex (UK, 1984)*

	Average duration of unemployment (months)	Unemployment rate
Age		
16–19	8.5	22.1
20–24	15.3	16.9
25–54	13.1	8.8
55–64	19.2	8.3
Race		
White	12.6	10.4
Other	17.6	20.1
Sex		
Male	16.1	11.2
Female	9.7	10.2

Source: *Unemployment* (Layard, Jackman and Nickell)

many countries, and suggests that policies aimed at reducing long-term unemployment, market mismatch and industry-level bargaining may reduce unemployment.

Further reading

For a general description of exchange rate regimes see *International Monetary Relations: Theory, History, and Policy* (Leland, G, Harper and Row, 1976). Issues surrounding the ERM are discussed in *Limiting Exchange Rate Flexibility: The European Monetary System* (Giavazzi, F and Giovannini, A, MIT Press, 1989).

The section on unemployment was drawn from *Unemployment* (Layard, R, Jackman, R and Nickell, S, OUP, 1991).

Glossary

Accelerator theory of investment   Explains the behaviour of corporate investment expenditure in terms of recent changes in output. Firms are assumed to project forward recent changes in activity so that, for example, a period of strong GDP growth raises their expectations of future output, causing them to raise capital expenditure. Since investment is part of GDP this will then lead to stronger activity and another round of increased investment, hence the term accelerator.

Aggregate demand   The total demand for an economy's goods and services.

Automatic stabilizers   Components of government spending and taxation (such as unemployment benefit) that respond automatically to the economic cycle. For example, if the economy is entering a recession, expenditure on benefits will automatically rise providing a fiscal boost which helps stabilize.

Balance of payments   Shows a country's transactions with the rest of the world and is divided into a current and capital account. The current account shows exports minus imports for both visible (goods) and invisible trade (services, net investment income and net transfers abroad). This is then matched by a flow of money on the capital account, either net borrowing to fund a current account deficit or net investment out of the country to offset a current account surplus.

Base money   Forms of money (such as notes and coins) which are only produced by the Central Bank. It is by controlling the supply of base money that Central Banks set interest rates.

Bilateral exchange rate   The exchange rate between two countries (eg the sterling/dollar exchange rate).

Constant returns to scale   Term used to describe the relationship between factor inputs (capital stock and labour force) and output where a 1 per cent increase in inputs results in a 1 per cent increase in output.

Consumers' expenditure   Spending by the personal sector on goods and services in a given period. It includes items such as cars, furniture, food, clothing, travel fares, rent and utility bills. It is often the largest component of GDP as measured from the expenditure side.

Cyclical deficit   The part of the budget deficit that is solely due to the state of the economy. Deficits automatically rise in recessions and fall in booms because of automatic stabilizers.

Deflator   Price index used to convert nominal values into real terms.

Domestic expenditure   The sum of consumer expenditure, government consumption, fixed investment and stockbuilding in a given period. Also known as domestic demand.

Econometric equation   A statistically estimated relationship which quantifies the impact of economic variables on one another.

Effective or trade weighted exchange rate   A measure of a country's exchange rate that takes a trade-weighted average of exchanges rates with its trading partners. The effective exchange rate provides a good summary measure of the influence of exchange rate movements on the economy.

Exports   Goods and services which are produced domestically but sold overseas.

Fiscal drag   The process by which government revenue tends to increase as a proportion of total output simply as a result of economic growth and/or inflation.

Fiscal neutrality   A fiscally neutral tax system is one that minimizes the distortions to economic decisions caused by taxation. It aims to reduce the incentive for people to make economic decisions simply to avoid or reduce their tax burden.

Fixed investment   Expenditure on capital items such as plant and equipment, roads and houses by both the public and private sectors. Represents the gross addition (ie before depreciation) to the economy's capital stock and helps determine the economy's potential output.

Forward market   A market where an investor can buy a given asset at a pre-arranged price for delivery some time in the future. For example, buying a three month sterling/dollar forward contract would give a UK investor a fixed amount of dollars at a pre-arranged exchange rate in three months time.

Fundamental equilibrium exchange rate (FEER) A measure of the exchange rate a country would need to have to bring its trade balance back into a sustainable equilibrium.

Government consumption Expenditure on health, education and other government services which are consumed by the public and generally paid for out of taxation.

Gross domestic product (GDP) The amount of goods and services produced by the economy in a given period. It is usually measured in real (ie volume) terms and is the most frequently quoted measure of economic activity. It can be calculated in three ways: directly from production in the economy; by adding up expenditure; or by totalling wages, salaries, rent and profits. The three measures should all produce the same value. The expenditure measure is the most frequently analysed and is equal to domestic expenditure plus exports and minus imports. Nominal GDP plus net interest, profits and rent received from abroad equals gross national product (GNP), which represents an economy's national income.

GDP at factor cost The expenditure measure of GDP at market prices, minus taxes plus subsidies.

GDP at market prices The expenditure measure of GDP (including taxes and subsidies).

Implied forward rate An expected level of short-term interest rates some time in the future. For instance, the 20 year implied forward rate would be the expected level of short-term interest rates in 20 years time. These rates can be derived from the yield curve.

Imports Goods and services which have been bought by domestic residents, but were produced overseas.

Inflation The percentage change in the price level over a given period, normally one year. Usually measured by taking the change in an index (such as the retail price index in the UK) which represents the price of a basket of goods and services which would be consumed by a typical household.

Involuntary unemployment People who are unemployed but who would be willing to take a job at the current market wage.

Macroeconomics   The study of the economy as a whole. It is primarily concerned with the amount the economy produces, how many people are employed in the process and how fast prices rise as a result.

Monetary base control   A method of setting monetary policy that is based on setting a quantity of base money and allowing interest rates to vary, rather than setting a level of interest rates and allowing base money to vary.

Multiplier effect   The effect through which a given change in government spending or taxation is multiplied so that its impact on GDP is bigger than the initial change.

Non-accelerating inflation rate of unemployment   The rate of unemployment (number of unemployed as a percent of the workforce) at which inflation is stable.

Open market operations   Market operations by the Central Bank that are used to set interest rates.

Optimal currency area   A group of countries that would benefit economically from fixing their currencies with one another.

Output gap   The difference between actual and potential GDP usually expressed as a percent of potential. When actual GDP is below potential the economy has a negative output gap, circumstances in which inflation normally falls. Conversely, when output is above potential there is a positive output gap and inflation rises.

Overnight interest rate   The interest rate received for investing money for one day only.

Phillips curve   A graphical relationship between unemployment and wage increases. If unemployment increases, there is more competition for work and wages tend to rise less rapidly. As unemployment falls, labour becomes more scarce and wages tend to accelerate. If a relationship between wages and prices has been specified, the Phillips curve can be shown in terms of unemployment and price inflation.

Potential output   The amount the economy can supply without causing inflation to accelerate. Calculated from the labour available, the capital stock and the efficiency with which they are combined (known as total factor productivity). Potential output is used to determine an economy's output gap and its long-run sustainable growth rate.

Public goods   Goods that are of benefit to many people but which no one individual would buy (eg National Defence). Public goods are better allocated by the government than by a free market.

Public sector borrowing requirement (PSBR)   A measure of how much the government needs to borrow to finance that part of its expenditure that is not financed by taxation.

Purchasing power parity (PPP)   A measure of the exchange rate that would need to hold to make goods in different countries cost the same.

Quantity identity   States that the stock of money in the economy multiplied by the number of times it circulates is equal to the total value of goods and services produced. As this is true by definition the relationship is known as an identity.

Real exchange rate   A measure of the exchange rate that adjusts for relative inflation across countries. A country with high inflation will have a rising real exchange rate because its goods are becoming more expensive overseas.

Real interest rate   The nominal rate of interest minus inflation. Real interest rates play an important part in determining consumers' expenditure and capital investment.

Real personal disposable Income (RPDI)   Nominal income of the personal sector after tax and adjusted for price increases. RPDI is a measure of real spending power and hence a key determinant of real consumer expenditure.

Recession   Period of falling activity, officially defined as two successive quarters of declining real GDP.

Replacement Ratio   The ratio of unemployment benefit to wages. The replacement ratio measures the increase in income that an unemployed person can get if they find a job.

Reserve Requirements   A legal obligation that requires commercial banks to hold a given proportion of their total deposits as Central Bank reserves. These requirements are used by some countries to increase the proportion of base money in total transactions money.

Seigniorage   The income the Central Bank derives from commercial banks holdings of non interest bearing base money (effectively an interest free loan to the Central Bank).

Stagflation   A dire situation where real GDP is falling but inflation continues to rise. Occurs when the economy is in recession but still operating above its potential.

Stockbuilding   Goods which have been produced but not sold. Stocks, or inventory, are included in the calculation of GDP even though they have not been bought, as they have still been produced by the economy.

Structural deficit   The part of the budget deficit that is due to longer run structural factors rather than changes in the economic cycle.

Term structure of interest rates   The relationship between long-term and short-term interest rates. The expectations theory of the term structure predicts that long-term interest rates are simply the average of expected future short-term rates over that period.

Transactions money   A measure of the money supply that attempts to include all forms of money used in transactions, including cash and bank accounts.

Total Factor Productivity   A term used to describe the efficiency with which labour and capital are combined. Captures the effects of new technology, better management techniques and improved education on potential output.

Uncovered interest parity (UIP)   A theory of exchange rate determination that predicts that a country's exchange rate will tend to fall if its interest rates are above those of other countries.

Velocity of circulation   The number of times that a unit of money is spent in a period. The velocity of circulation defines the relationship between the money supply and actual output.

Yield curve   The relationship between interest rates of different maturity shown graphically as a curve. The slope of the curve is useful for predicting interest rates in the future and changes in real GDP.

BIBLIOGRAPHY

Alesina, A (1989) 'Politics and business cycles in industrial democracies', *Economic Policy*, volume 8.

Alesina, A and Summers, L (1993) 'Central bank independence and macroeconomic performance: some comparative evidence', *Journal of Money Credit and Banking*, May.

Blanchard, O (1987) 'Reaganomics', *Economic Policy*, volume 5.

Buiter, W (1985) 'A guide to public sector debt and deficits', *Economic Policy*, volume 1.

Dornbusch, R and Layard, R (eds.) (1987), *The Performance of the British Economy*, Oxford University Press, Oxford.

Giavazzi, F and Spaventa, L (1988) *High Public Debt: the Italian Experience*, Cambridge University Press, Cambridge.

Giavazzi, F and Giovannini, A (1989) *Limiting Exchange Rate Flexibility: The European Monetary System*, MIT Press, Cambridge, MA.

Goodhart, C (1989) *Money information and uncertainty*, MIT Press, Cambridge, MA.

Institute of Economic Affairs (1990) *The State of the Economy.*

Kay, J and King, M (1986) *The UK Tax System*, Oxford University Press, Oxford.

Layard, R, Jackman, R and Nickell, S (1991) *Unemployment*, Oxford University Press, Oxford.

Leland, H (1976) *International relations: Theory, History and Policy*, Harper and Row, USA.

MacFarlane, H and Mortimer-Lee, P (1994) 'Inflation over the last 300 years', *Bank of England Quarterly Bulletin*, May.

Malkiel, B (1981) *A Random Walk Down Wall Street*, Norton, New York.

Mankiw, G (1994) *Macroeconomics*, Worth.

Muellbauer, J and Murphy, P (1990) 'Is the UK balance of payments sustainable?', *Economic Policy*, volume 5.

National Institute Economic Review, *Consumption and Borrowing: An assessment of recent personal sector behavior in the UK*, 3/94.

Nickell, S (1978) *The Investment Decisions of Firms*, Oxford University Press, Oxford.

Oxford Review of Economic Policy, *Inflation*, Winter 1990.

Oxford Review of Economic Policy (1994) *Consumption*.

Swiss Bank Corporation (1987) *Foreign Exchange and money market operations*.

Wyplosz, P and Burda, M (1993) *Macroeconomics: A European text*, Oxford University Press, Oxford.

Index

shocks 46–7
surveys
    business 117
    CBI *Industrial Trends* 106, 108,
        111, 117
    data sources 124
    INSEE, France 105

taxation 54–6
    import regimes 93
    increases 62
    revenue 53
TFP *see* total factor productivity
total factor productivity (TFP) 39
trade
    imports and exports 18, 30, 94,
        105, 117
    non-traded goods 93
    stability 127
trade-weighted 87–8
    exchange rate 94
transactions money 72–3

UIP *see* uncovered interest parity
UK 130
    economy 108–9
    exchange rate 95
    exports 76
    Growth Forecast 119–20
    interest rates 76
    money targeting 74–5

official reports 124
uncovered interest parity (UIP)
    89–91, 98
underlying inflation 107
unemployment 134–8
    benefit system 135–7
    involuntary 134
    NAIRU 44
    natural rate 44
US
    Central Bank 98
    dollars 87, 129
    report, National Association of
        Purchasing Managers 104

velocity of circulation 73
Very Short Term Financing Facility
    (VSTF) 130
Vietnam war 129
volatility 127
Volker, Paul 98

wage determination 134–5
wage-bargaining systems 135
wealth 116
world demand 32, 118

yield curves 79, 112–13

zero inflation 73